My Courage to Tell

to Tell

Facing a Childhood Bully and

Reclaiming my Inner Child

Revised Edition

LAURA E. CORBETH

Printed in United States of America

Revised Edition, 2019

ISBN 978-1-7750198-3-1

For information contact :
www.lauracorbeth.com

Book and Cover design by the author.

The author of *My Courage to Tell* is not a clinical psychologist or a psychotherapist. This her truthful life story about being terrorized by her brother's cruel behaviour, while her parents were complicit by allowing it to continue.

If this book can help one person recognize the symptoms and patterns of abuse, it will have accomplished its mission and design. This book is NOT and should NOT be considered for legal or clinical advice. Rather, it is to help others who may be trapped in terrible situations unable to understand whom and what they are dealing with. For help, always consult your family doctor who will recommend a trained professional. There is help available, but you need to recognize the patterns first.

There have been few books written from a sibling's perspective about the effects of consistent cruel treatment by a sibling with predatory behaviour. You are about to read one.

This is the story of the author becoming a survivor.

Hopefully it is helpful.

The author has met with multiple clinical psychologists who have drawn the same conclusions based on her experiences and story – that the patterns and behaviour the author experienced were psychologically and physically abusive.

WITH AN EXTRA SPECIAL THANKS
TO MY HUSBAND AND SON FOR THEIR
CONTINUED LOVE AND SUPPORT.
I AM BLESSED TO HAVE YOU IN MY LIFE.

THIS BOOK IS DEDICATED TO
MY INNER CHILD, LITTLE LAURA
WHO IS COURAGEOUS
AND NOW WANTS TO TELL.

Forward

LAURA REALLY DOES SOMETHING INCREDIBLE with this book. She finds the strength and courage to tell a story about abuse – a story that will be all too familiar for millions of men and women – a story that often never gets told. She shines a spotlight on an area that demands our attention. Her brave account of suffering psychological abuse at the hands of an older brother, under the watchful eyes of her mother, is heartbreaking, riveting and empowering. It is a story that needs to be told.

Psychological and emotional abuse (terms I use interchangeably) are often misunderstood, minimized, or ignored. Over the past decade alone, there have been substantial advances with respect to identifying, preventing and treating those who have suffered sexual and physical abuse; however, there has been much less attention to identifying and addressing psychological abuse. Defined, psychological abuse is an intentional pattern of behaviour in which one individual exerts control over another through very systematic and specific means. People often assume that emotional abuse primarily consists of yelling, screaming, name-calling, constant criticisms or put downs; it is assumed that the abuse would be so obvious and palpable that the victim would seek help and/or others would notice and express concern. While this may be the case in some situations, emotional abuse is often much more insidious and covert. Consistent with Laura's writing, victims are subjected to a chronic pattern of intimidation, lack of empathy and support, gaslighting (e.g., making a person feel "crazy" by making them doubt their memories and experiences), subtle and overt threats to safety, financial abuse and isolation. Such behaviour can be verbal (e.g., sarcasm, under-the-breath comments) and non-verbal (e.g., silent treatment, grimacing, glaring).

One of the most frightening aspects of dealing with an emotionally abusive person is their ability to charm others, lie or speak only in half-truths, blame the victim for any difficulties and/or minimize the concerns of the victim when he or she does speak up. One of the most difficult and painful aspects of Laura's story is her realization of the way her parents and family members reinforced her brother's abusive acts by NOT acting, by minimizing Laura's repeated attempts for safety and by chalking it up to "sibling rivalry". Sadly, it is not uncommon for members of the family to support, defend and even glorify the abusive party. This is especially confusing for a child who looks to his/her parent(s) to protect them. In Laura's case, she was threatened that she would be killed if she told – and yet, when she finally mustered up the courage to tell in her early years, she was not believed and was, at times, made to feel shame for speaking up. A child will withdraw, tend to blame him or herself and suffer in silence.

The impact of living in a psychologically abusive home or relationship is harmful for anyone and when a child grows up in such an environment, the results are even more damaging. Studies have shown that adverse childhood experiences (ACES) that include emotional abuse, neglect and lack of proper supervision (among others) of children can impact brain development and are associated with a greater likelihood of developing chronic health problems, being diagnosed with a mental health disorder (e.g., anxiety, eating disorders, depression and suicidal behaviours), having behavioural problems and difficulty with emotion dysregulation, and having a greater likelihood of premature death. Victims typically have low self-esteem, forever doubting their value, recollections and "gut" instincts. ("I know something is wrong, but no one else seems to notice...is it just me?") They develop maladaptive beliefs about themselves ("I am unlovable"), the world ("I cannot trust anyone") and the future ("I will never be safe"). Without understanding the pattern of abuse and/or working through their trauma in treatment, victims often feel forever imprisoned in their fear and doubt.

My Courage to Tell makes the invisible visible. Reading Laura's account of healing and recovery is inspirational and is an outstanding contribution to the literature on psychological abuse in families. Her willingness to confront and share the scary and painful reality of her childhood and detail how various treatment interventions allowed her to work through distressing memories, emotions, and beliefs will pave the way for others who recognize themselves in Laura's story. This is a story about hope, resilience and strength for anyone experiencing psychological abuse.

Anita Federici, Ph.D
Clinical Psychologist

Prologue

I T'S CHRISTMAS TIME – one of my favourite times of the year. Everything just shines and glitters. It's a time to be with friends and family. A time of cheer. Looking at our white angel at the top of our tree, she represents so much to me. She has been there for my twenty-one married years. She's old but looks beautiful holding her little lit candle in her hands. Her eyes are closed and she has a look of peace on her face. It looks like she is blessing me and my life.

This angelic figure represents years of celebration with my husband, James, and son, Mitchell. A wonderful, loving, and supportive husband. An unbelievable son whom both my husband and I cherish.

I look at her and remember the many years of excitement of "Santa" coming. In the morning, Mitchell would wake up with the anticipation of receiving his gifts from magical St. Nick who had placed them carefully underneath the tree waiting to be opened. Over the years, presents were also waiting to be opened from our rescued dogs and cat.

Our house is decorated with beautiful ornaments that we have collected over the years. Christmas is a chance to celebrate our hard work and be grateful for all we have.

Looking at that angelic light at the top of my tree, I think of how blessed I am. But this was not always so.

I was seven years old. Our family had finally purchased a house. We had immigrated from Scotland two years earlier. This was the third house we had lived in since immigrating to Canada. Each house had been in a completely different neighbourhood, so making friends was difficult. I was a full-blown introvert, in full retreat.

My brother was three years older than me. I had always desperately wanted his love, but I didn't get it. What I did get was continuous bullying, intimidation, threats on my safety and terrible mental and physical abuse. I had endured many threats on my life, if I ever told my parents what he was doing. There was no support or protection, and my only sibling, my brother, knew it. I was an easy target.

My brother wanted to find the Christmas presents that were hidden somewhere in the house. "Come on. Let's go look for the presents," he said. He was being nice to me. My brother always had two faces. This was the nice face that most people got to see when he wanted something from them. "Alright," I replied, desperately seeking his approval. I didn't really want to find the presents, but being the good follower that I was, I participated.

Our house was very small, so we didn't have to look too many places to find them. We had very little furniture. There was the main floor with three bedrooms, a bathroom, a living room and tiny kitchen. The basement was unfinished.

We looked on the main floor. We looked everywhere. They weren't there. So down we went to the basement. Our family had a large brown chest that stood up on its side with a huge door on the front. It was massive in size compared to me. We opened it. BAM! There they were. All the presents that Mom had bought to be wrapped for Christmas. We saw them all. All the gifts that were to be a wonderful surprise on Christmas morning were found. Christmas, that wonderful time of year for children, was ruined.

Mom came home. We told her the "good" news. She was so hurt and completely devastated. In order to try and save Christmas, Mom decided to give us a present each day. At the very least, we didn't know which present was coming. Trying to make it okay, she told us it would be like Hanukkah. My father was Jewish and Mom was a Christian. Mom had taught us a little bit about the Jewish religion, so I had a sense of what Hanukkah was.

I remember one of my presents was a beautiful perfume bottle. I loved it very much. Such a nice present for a little girl of my age. It wasn't glass like a normal perfume bottle. It was similar to a bottle of hair mousse. You couldn't see what was inside the bottle. And just like a mousse bottle, you could shake it.

That night I laid in bed. I put my hands together and prayed, "Dear Jesus, thank you so much for my perfect gift. It is beautiful." My family wasn't religious at all but I was a very spiritual little girl. Always grateful for anything I was given. I had never attended church, but had a picture of Jesus on my dresser. I somehow loved this man from two thousand years ago. Maybe it's because I was told he loved children.

I put my beautiful new gift on my dresser next to the picture. In the morning I planned to use the perfume and smell very pretty and beautiful. I closed my eyes in anticipation of the morning.

I was drifting off for my night's sleep when my brother quietly snuck into my bedroom. He was crawling on his knees. My parents were asleep. I opened my eyes, "What are you doing?" I asked innocently. "Shhhhh! Be *quiet!*" he whispered angrily. He showed me his other face. The one of hate and anger that I was used to. The one with the cross eyebrows, squinted eyes and lips pressed tightly together.

He took the new Christmas bottle from my dresser and shook it violently. He then carefully placed it at the bottom of my bed next to my feet. "Don't you *dare* move or it will blow up," he threatened, making sure my parents hadn't heard him. "It's a *bomb* and if you move it will go off and blow you to pieces," he added, with such meaning and hate in his voice.

I was terrified of moving. I was frozen. Scared to death. I was always so trusting, so I believed him. Then he gritted his teeth and looked at me, enraged. "Don't you dare tell or I'll *kill* you!" I believed that too. I had seen him kill and torment animals. Why not me?

This was one of his many threats to kill me if I ever told anyone what he was doing. I didn't sleep well that night. And, I held it in and didn't tell. He'd kill me if I did.

Chapter 1

Memories of Terror

Children who are emotionally abused and neglected face similar and sometimes worse mental health problems as children who are physically or sexually abused, yet psychological abuse is rarely addressed in prevention programs or in treating victims, according to a new study published by the American Psychological Association.

—American Psychological Association, 2014

I T WAS A VOICE I HADN'T heard in fifty years. A little girl's voice that was silenced. I met her when I started my intense therapy a few years ago. It was then that I was diagnosed with Post-Traumatic Stress Disorder.

Little Laura was terrified. She had to live with threats. She learned to live with a bully who got pleasure from his control and abuse. Most people want to come home to a safe haven. She came home to a family member who constantly threatened her life, using fear to control her. Her sibling who looked for ways to see her suffer and cry. It gave him the pleasure to see her pain. He hated her.

The worst memories were the threats on her safety. Living with terror, every day, that something might happen to her if she told. "If you *ever* tell, you'll be sorry. I'll *get* you," he said in his threatening way while gritting his teeth. "I will *kill* you." The threat was real to her.

She wrote me that she felt terrorized. She travelled in the car – her bully was there. She ate at the kitchen table – her bully was there. This little five-year-old girl, Little Laura, told me that she had to walk to school with her bully. At school, her bully, with his predatory behaviour, was there. Every day. Feeling terrorized was something this little girl learned to live with.

There were the lies. They were continuous. He would lie and no one was the wiser. She would complain of his bullying to her mom. "No I'm not," he'd lie with a snicker and shake his head. "She's making it up. She's *lying again* Mom," he'd say convincingly. "She's *always* making things up!" He was *really* good at the lying.

Her mother never knew who was lying. Then, he'd look at her with a smirk.

This little girl wrote me how frustrated she was. She would grit her teeth until they hurt. She'd plead her case trying to get her mother to believe she was telling the truth. It went on deaf ears.

Manipulations were unrestrained. Sometimes her mother would say something to her brother for bullying her. "Now, *cut* it out," she'd say. There was an immediate reply, "You're *always* taking her side." Or she heard, "You love *her* more than me." He knew very well how to manipulate her mother.

Then there was the physical abuse. There was the unique ability to use his superficial charm, coupled with an insincere giggle to excuse what he was doing to her, saying it was nothing. "I was *only tickling* her," smirking smugly while he said it. "She makes such a big deal about *everything*." He could hold her down, against her will, and do anything to her that he wanted. Spitting. Licking. Tickling. As long as I didn't end up with a bruise or a cut, there were no issues. He knew the rules.

It was abuse that was invisible.

Her parents turned a blind eye. With most complaints, Little Laura was lumped together with her brother – the bully. "Both of you stop it, right now. Just stop this nonsense." Nothing would happen. There were never any consequences for teasing or tormenting her.

She told me how she was always laughed at. Her pain was a "joke". Everything was always a joke. She didn't find her pain so funny.

And then there were the animals. She witnessed the tormenting, torturing, skinning and killing of live animals. The terror of her brother was very real. She saw what he was capable of.

Could she run away? No! If she ran away, she'd have to say why. She'd have to tell. She had moved so many times, she had no family around that she could confide in. She had no friends. She felt completely – and utterly – alone.

She was trapped.

I don't know how that little girl got through those abusive years. The terror years. I just don't know. A little girl with no protection. All by herself. Living every day with a constant threat. Controlled by the use of fear. It was frightening. Terrifying.

She wrote me a few years ago and her first words thanked me.

"Hi. I am glad you are here. Thanks for helping me," she wrote calling out to me.

It broke my heart.

These are the memories I chose to forget until my Aunt Vanna died two years ago. It all changed then.

Chapter 2

Aunt Vanna

MY AUNT VANNA WAS A VERY interesting and eccentric person. She lived an extremely secretive existence. She was a larger-than-life personality. She was often abrasive, forceful, even rude – a typical New Yorker. My aunt was an Emmy-Award winning producer and writer. After her death, we discovered a great deal more about Aunt Vanna that no one could have ever imagined. There's more to everyone than meets the eye, I guess.

Aunt Vanna was my father's younger sister and the middle child of three siblings. My father was five years older than her, and Vanna's sister was a year and a half younger. Aunt Vanna played a significant part in this story and I suppose in my life. Without Vanna, her eventual passing and all that transpired with her estate, I might never have begun to understand the abuse that I experienced as a child. And, I might not have ever faced my abuser.

Aunt Vanna had left Scotland for Canada ten years before my family did. Her quest to rise from poverty led her to seek a new life in a different country. My family followed her, also looking for a "better life". We were all trying to escape and overcome the harsh beginnings of the *Gorbals*. As a young child, moving to a new country with my family was difficult for me. I can only imagine how hard it was for my aunt, who left on her own when she was only seventeen.

***

The Gorbals, the concrete jungle of Glasgow's slums, were not a place any of us can imagine living in. It was the 1930s and there was a housing shortage at the time. Living standards were very low and street gangs, rats, immigrants and overcrowding were everywhere evident. Photographs of the Gorbals show little children running in mud with their clothes spattered in the dirt. There were approximately 85,000 people living in the Gorbals at that time.

In the back of the buildings, the playgrounds were the stone alleys, along with the middens. The middens were the concrete structures similar to garages. They had no doors and contained all the food waste. Plastic bags were a thing of the future, so the middens were a great attraction for rats.

To get to a park, the family had to pay for a tram that would take them to somewhere they might see some greenery. But it didn't happen often.

It was tight living quarters for the family of five who shared a two-bedroom apartment. An old black stove with a coal fire had a dual purpose. One, to heat the small space and, two, to cook the food. The family was lucky enough to have a toilet of their own. Many units in the tenements had no bathroom at all and there would be a need to share the common bathroom in the stairwell. The family toilet was in a tiny, separate room without a sink. The room was so small. There was a little step leading up to the toilet and just enough room to turn around and close the door once you entered. At the time, for many, a newspaper was the only choice for toilet paper, but the family was also fortunate enough to have real toilet paper. It wasn't soft like the toilet paper we know today. It was more like tracing paper.

The simple pleasure of hot running water was non-existent. The one sink, with cold water, was in the kitchen. It also had a dual purpose – washing the dishes and daily bathing, first thing in the morning. Everyone would take turns. Once a week, the family would go to the communal public baths that had very little hot water. Both my aunts would have to share the same bath.

The everyday luxuries of comfortable couches and chairs were unheard of. The kitchen was the common area with a table and hard chairs. On the table would sit the radio, the only form of communication from the outside world.

Dirty clothes were brought to public wash houses called *steamies*. The clothes would then be carried home and hung to dry in the kitchen from a line with a pulley on the ceiling. They would drip-dry over all the kitchen chairs where everyone would sit.

Owning a cat was important back in the Gorbals. Cats were great for catching the mice that were rampant in the apartments. One time, my Aunt Vanna came home with a little white kitten in her arms. The kitten was sick. She wanted to keep it. My grandmother said, "There is no way we can keep that kitten. We do not have the money for a vet." My aunt replied, "I'm keeping him and taking him to the vet myself." I'm not sure whatever happened to that poor little kitten, but when I heard this story, I realized Aunt Vanna had a heart for animals.

It is hard to imagine living in the Gorbals in today's world. We live in luxury and we don't even know it.

Vanna had a lot of hardship to overcome from her early years. Born with a very large nose and talking with a terrible stutter, children made fun of her. Also, an unfortunate accident, while running down a hill and ramming into a railing, had ended with my poor aunt losing her two front teeth. She had been given two non-complementary false teeth. Dental implants were a thing of the future.

Vanna was sent to a special boarding school for her stammer and was taught to sing and slow her speech down. She overcame her stuttering. It must have been a huge accomplishment for her, in her adult years, to narrate an Emmy Award-winning film.

Even as a child, my Aunt Vanna had an argumentative nature. She and her sister argued daily. It was constant warfare. Vanna would bully her younger sister and always encouraged her older brother, my father, to participate. Vanna had a lot of hate for her pretty younger sister and seemed to have a big chip on her shoulder.

From a young age, my aunt cared very much about money. Desperately wanting to move to Canada, Aunt Vanna was a bit of a miser, saving every cent she could make. And, when she was seventeen, that happened. All the money she had saved for years was used to pay for her ticket. She packed her bag and took the long ship ride across the ocean, all by herself, destined for Canada. It was pretty courageous for a young woman of that age to venture to a new country as she did. I heard that everyone was yelling to my aunt when she was waving goodbye, "Take your teeth out if you get seasick!" Poor Vanna. That must have been humiliating.

Vanna arrived safely in Canada. She had arranged to stay with my grandmother's sister, her Auntie Rachel. Auntie Rachel had sponsored her niece to come to Canada and prepared a room for her. She had thrown an old mattress down on the floor. That was it. Not a kind-hearted person, to say the least. As you can imagine, Aunt Vanna clashed with her aunt and she decided, a year later, to move to New York City where another relative had sponsored her. Vanna was determined to find a home that could offer her opportunity.

By her early 20s, my aunt rented a six-hundred square foot one-bedroom apartment in Greenwich Village, a very popular, trendy area of Manhattan in the '60s. She had begun working for PBS on a children's program and had become a real New Yorker. She was even more belligerent and argumentative than she used to be. You didn't *ever* want to pick a fight with her. You'd lose.

Aunt Vanna had a strong presence about her. When entering a room, she commanded your attention. She seemed to have it "all together". An avid reader and investigator, reading multiple newspapers a day, she always knew what was happening. Aunt Vanna was always up on her politics and she followed all the new, innovative health remedies.

Vanna was more exotic than attractive. After arriving in New York, she changed her looks with some plastic surgery and dental work. Her nose, that kids had made fun of, was reconstructed. She replaced her false teeth with some new, shiny, white implants. The false teeth were gladly thrown away. Vanna walked with complete confidence and with a spring in her step. She was on top of the world, a long way from being a stuttering, insecure child in the Gorbals.

***

Ten years after Aunt Vanna left, my family moved to Canada. Not long after we moved, my Aunt Adena, Aunt Vanna's younger sister, and my grandmother came to New York City and Canada for a holiday. First stop – New York City. They flew into LaGuardia airport. After their long eight-hour flight, their own helicopter awaited them. It picked them up and flew them directly into Manhattan, right onto the top the Pan Am building. After they landed, my aunt met them at the bottom of the building. It seemed that Aunt Vanna was doing *really* well. She spent little time with her visitors. She arranged for them to see the Broadway shows, *Fiddler on the Roof* and *Man of La Mancha*. She spent little time with her mother and sister before they left for Canada. My Aunt Vanna was cold and had become fiercely independent and very successful, it seemed.

When I was only seven years old and my brother was ten we flew by ourselves to New York City. Aunt Vanna took us to her office at

PBS and we played while she was busy working during the day. I walked into a big open loft-type office with lots of windows and seeing big boxes of toys. There were dolls of all kinds. My brother saw a box of G.I. Joes and army trucks. We were thrilled. My aunt said we could keep the toys. This was so amazing to me.

After our weekend visit, we packed up and got ready to drive back to Canada. Vanna had bought a small Porsche, which obviously wasn't ideal for a long trip with children. We loaded up the car. With the two boxes of toys, there wasn't much room and we had a big drive ahead of us. On our way, I couldn't lie down in the back seat and I was complaining. My aunt couldn't take it. She had no patience. She pulled over to the side of the highway. "Each of you can pick a toy," she said sternly. Then she said, "One toy. The rest will be left at the side of the road. I will not put up with this whining." I was devastated. I loved my new toys. We drove off and I looked back at the boxes as we drove away.

But it was such a dichotomy. We saw Porsches and helicopters, but Aunt Vanna was always crying poor. She continued to live in her rent-controlled apartment, bought second-hand clothing and costume jewelry. She always was asking others to pay for her lunch and dinner. When she travelled home to see her ageing parents, she would ask for money. Nobody really could tell what she was. Was she poor or rich? One thing that she definitely was, was strange. Eccentric.

My Aunt Vanna would come and visit us quite often in Canada. She was very close to my father. But visits were always strained and difficult. My mother would always brace herself for the visits. They were never pleasant. The first question she would ask when she heard that Vanna was coming was, "How long is she staying?" And when she left, there was always a sigh of relief. My aunt was so antagonistic. Challenging everyone and trying to cause arguments gave her great pleasure. She was so self-righteous and everyone else was always wrong.

Aunt Vanna was also a big health food fanatic. She would take multiple vitamin pills each day and on her visits, she would criticize my mom on how we were eating. A few of Vanna's friends had died of cancer, and she was a big reader on the potential causes of cancer and what to eat to prevent the disease. She always boasted that she'd never needed to see a doctor or dentist and about how healthy she was.

Along with her arrogant nature, my aunt did have some kind of charisma. Husbands, who were friends of our family, would flock to her and their wives would wonder what it was that men liked about her. My mother could never understand it. She disliked her sister-in-law and couldn't see what anyone would like about her.

My aunt's biggest accomplishment was her involvement in a contentious documentary. The controversial film earned her an Emmy Award. She was the co-producer, writer and narrator. Pictures of her on stage, receiving her Emmy with the glitzy Hollywood stars, amazed me. She seemed so strong and successful, or so I thought.

CHAPTER 3.

VANNA AND ME

THE WEEKEND TOUR

AS TIME PASSED, MY AUNT AND I kept in touch. I always heard how she was doing through my father who spoke to her every week. Dad and Vanna were always close and even more so when my parents divorced after twenty-five years of marriage.

When I was in my late twenties, I decided to take a visit to New York and stay with my aunt. I told Vanna to just take me around the city and show me what she wanted me to see. I didn't want the visit to be all about me.

I arranged for the flight.

"Just take a cab when you get here, and I'll meet you at the apartment. Oh, and bring your running shoes," Vanna said to me before my trip.

Not being a traveller, I insisted on her meeting me at the airport. I was nervous about going to such a big city. Vanna respected my request and met me when I landed. I was so glad she had, as I felt pretty uncomfortable upon arrival. A small town girl from Canada visiting the big metropolis of New York City.

We took a cab to Vanna's place in mid-Manhattan and the cab dropped us off.

We walked up the stairs. Vanna opened up the six bolted locks on her door. I looked at her wondering why she had so many locks. I was not used to this much security.

Vanna's apartment was small but organized. Her book collection took up most of the wall space on one side and her record collection took up the wall space on the other side. I agreed to sleep on the couch.

We stayed in that night and talked. Vanna showed me her prized record collection that was worth thousands of dollars. It was full of old jazz records and we listened to Ella Fitzgerald all night.

"You had such terrible parents when you were a child," she said to me in a serious tone.

"I did?" I questioned Vanna. I was not really sure if I believed her. Vanna was always so negative.

"We never anticipated your parents' marriage lasting as long as it did," she continued.

I just listened to Vanna speak badly about my family and decided not to make anything of it. I let her opinion go in one ear and out the other. I knew she really didn't talk positively about anyone.

While we were talking, I heard "POP. POP." Then some yelling outside.

"What the hell was that?" I questioned.

Vanna walked over to the window and looked out.

"Gunshots," she replied smiling.

"Oh come on!" I was in disbelief.

She laughed and shook her head. New York was very different than where I grew up.

My aunt seemed happy. She had retired decades before and didn't work. I had many questions but didn't ask them. There was a theme in my family – never ask questions. So, I never discussed my aunt's past work with her. And, I never asked her why she was always alone. Aunt Vanna never had a relationship with anyone her whole life. Family rumours and gossip had left me wondering. I was curious but I had always respected people's privacy, so I didn't ask the questions that were on my mind.

"So you just want to see the city?"

"Just show me how you live in New York," I responded. I couldn't wait to see the action of New York City. "I've brought my running shoes as you suggested."

Vanna told me to get ready for the next day, as she was going to take me everywhere on foot. I was heavy into working out and thought I'd have no problem keeping up with Aunt Vanna who was in her fifties.

We woke up and got ready. The sun was shining. It was a brilliant day.

I was putting on my makeup and Vanna came over with some new cream for under my eyes. She told me to put it on because it would help with my wrinkles. I did as she told me, then we talked about where we would go.

I was excited.

We both put on our running shoes and ventured out. Vanna wore one of her loose, flowered dresses from the sixties. We started on our hike through Manhattan.

We first ventured down to Wall Street and the financial district. It was going to be our first stop.

We started to walk towards the Twin Towers. They were monstrous buildings. The day was warm and sunny and I really enjoyed just looking around at building upon building.

"That's where Robert DeNiro lives," Vanna told me. She pointed to a low rise building. He was only a few blocks away. "His place is the whole second floor of that building."

"You're kidding," I marvelled.

It led to a conversation about Bill Cosby.

"He is a very bad guy you know," she smirked. Vanna said everything with a purpose.

"What do you mean?" I asked her.

She didn't elaborate, but looked at me and opened her eyes and rolled them. She knew something that she chose not to share. I was taken aback at the names she was mentioning.

We got to Wall Street and the Trade Centre within minutes and then we rode the elevator to the top of the Twin Towers. When we arrived at the top, I couldn't believe the sight. The whole of Manhattan was in view. We walked all around the top of the building and my aunt pointed out all the buildings and landmarks.

"That's The Empire State Building; Statue of Liberty; the Hudson River; and New Jersey just across the river," Vanna boasted pointing at all the buildings.

You could see everything! Aunt Vanna loved the city and she was so proud when showing it to me.

"This is really cool." I was impressed.

I took picture upon picture as I walked around the massive building.

We left and ventured over to the Pier 15 Esplanade on the East River. There was a person all dressed up as the Statue of Liberty and the area was so lively. It was a happy place. I took more pictures.

We sat and had a drink, and then we were off again. We walked along the waterfront and then to Canal Street for some second-hand shopping. We finally landed in Chinatown for authentic Chinese food.

My aunt ordered Dim Sum which I didn't really like. I just wanted the Chicken Balls and Chicken Fried Rice. Aunt Vanna rolled her eyes and laughed at me. My small town ways gave her a chuckle.

My aunt was incredibly fit and had so much energy. I have to admit she out-walked me. We headed back to her apartment and I got ready for the next day. I massaged my feet and slept solidly after our very active day.

When I woke up, Vanna phoned an elderly lady in the building. She wanted to know if she needed any food.

"Do you need me to get you anything?" Vanna asked the woman on the phone.

I waited to hear what Vanna wanted to do. She hung up.

"This neighbour has a hard time getting around and can't get out for her groceries."

There was another softer side to my aunt that people didn't see. It seemed to me that Vanna was much happier without people around and in her own space. She wasn't trying to impress anyone.

The lady in the building said she was fine, so we headed off to Brooklyn. We needed to take the subway to get to the parade that was going on that day. When we walked down to the subway, a man urinated right in front of me. I looked over at my aunt with disbelief. She didn't even seem to notice.

We arrived and watched the West Indian Day Parade in Brooklyn. Everyone was enjoying themselves as were we. It was a great time. We ventured back to Manhattan to a fruit market where one of Vanna's friends had a fruit stand that also sold honey. She said she volunteered to help him sometimes. We worked together and I met more New Yorkers. I enjoyed seeing and meeting the people that lived there, up close and personal.

It was an action-packed trip and I went back home completely exhausted.

***

A few years passed and I met my husband. My husband, James,

was quite the opposite of my family. He said things like they were and he was outspoken to a fault. He was a fighter. He would tell people to their face if they *pissed* him off. James didn't cause arguments, but, if you disrespect him, he would let you know.

I heard from my father that Aunt Vanna was coming for a visit. James and I were engaged at the time and had just started living together. Dad asked if I would pick her up from the airport and let her stay with us for a few days. Dad lived three hours away in a small town north of where we lived. He was semi-retired and worked weekends for some extra income. He had to work at the flea market and it was going to be a busy weekend for him.

Unfortunately, Dad always had blinders on when it came to his sister Vanna. I was very reluctant. I knew what my aunt was like. Aggressive, belligerent and extremely opinionated. My inside voice was screaming, *NO WAY!* But, being a people pleaser, I agreed and braced myself for the weekend.

I tried to warn James about how difficult a person my aunt was, but few people could prepare for such a trying and uncooperative person.

***

We picked Aunt Vanna up at the airport. She got in the car and it started immediately. She started complaining about everything. The flight was terrible and the flight attendants gave her a hard time. My aunt travelled light. She had brought her small black carry-on bag along with a used kitchen pot that she wanted to give to us. The flight attendants gave her problems about the space she needed.

It seemed like a big black cloud was hanging above her head and was following her around. I looked over at James. His eyes said it all. Five minutes in and we were already uncomfortable. I thought, *How the hell am I going to get through this?*

We got back to our condo. It was the most beautiful place that I had ever lived in. We were on the twenty-third floor and, with floor to ceiling glass, it overlooked the city and airport. At night it was just glorious. Lights had glittered everywhere. I was thinking my aunt would be impressed, but I thought wrong.

"I have friends in White Plains, New York that have a place much nicer than this," she said to me in her opinionated voice.

"Great," I said, feeling a little slighted.

"You have no idea," she replied back.

Vanna sat down and couldn't wait to talk to me about her sister. She was seething with anger. My Aunt Adena had married Vanna's best friend's husband. Vanna's friend had suffered for a year and a half, fighting her battle with cancer, before she passed away. It wasn't quite a year afterward, that her widowed husband married Vanna's sister. I tried to understand, but, personally, I didn't see what the problem was. Two people that found love. I suspected that this feud had started way back in the Gorbals.

I looked through the newspapers to see if there were any good garage sales on for the weekend. My aunt didn't like to pay full price for anything and enjoyed rummaging through garage sales to try and find something that could be worth money. Off we went for the afternoon.

After we were finished combing a few of the sales, we travelled over to my mother and her husband's house. It was to be a quick visit for them to say hello.

My aunt walked in and brought her insults and negativity with her. It was embarrassing. I am sure my mother was quite happy when we left. Aunt Vanna was insulting them on their lifestyle and everything my mother was doing wrong. Some things never change.

We headed home and I sat in the car wondering how much longer I could take her company. She was so negative and exasperating. Was Vanna trying to prove something to James whom she'd never met? Maybe. I didn't know. All I knew is that people had always "put up" with her antics, but James's patience was wearing thin.

When we arrived home, Vanna walked over to the couch and took off her socks. She continued talking about my mother and her new husband. She was not impressed. She then turned her socks inside out and snapped them on her hands, to try and get the dirt out of them. Dust and dirt flew everywhere in the sunlight. I think our complete surprise showed.

One more day, I thought. We went to bed.

"I'm going to work tomorrow. I just can't take her anymore," James stated.

"Okay, Babe," I answered. "She'll be leaving tomorrow."

I went to sleep thinking about how my aunt's visit had been so stressful.

Sunday morning arrived.

Vanna was sleeping in our spare room where our books were openly displayed on the bookshelves. She came out with a book in her hand. It was a book from a mayor of New York City that she did not like very much.

"Why would you read a book from such a criminal?" she snapped accusingly to James, questioning him on his book choice.

"I read all sorts of books," he stated.

I thought, *Oh God, here we go.* Vanna started her attacks with James. I wanted to run and hide because I could see where this was going. Vanna liked to cause arguments and James would not take it.

"He's an asshole and you shouldn't be buying a book from such a person," she scolded.

"Whether he is an asshole or not, it's really none of your business what I read," James replied in frustration.

I had never seen anyone challenge my aunt and her pushy ways. She walked off in a huff.

Vanna headed off into the shower and James was heading out. I thought I had almost made it through the weekend. It was Sunday, and my cousin was going to pick up my aunt later to take Vanna to my father's cottage.

Vanna was in the bathroom for a very long time. She was taking forever. I had no idea what she was doing. I listened to hear when she finished her shower. James desperately needed his brush. He waited as long as he could, but eventually, I had to knock on the bathroom door.

"Aunt Vanna, could you please pass me the big round brush underneath the sink?"

There was a long pause. Finally, she passed it out of the door, not showing her face. Oh, Lord. It was wet and full of her long black hair. Oh no! That was it. James threw the brush.

"That's it! She has to go!" he yelled. James left.

It was definitely time for Aunt Vanna to leave. I made arrangements for her to be picked up by her cousin earlier than expected.

My father phoned me when my aunt arrived. He was angry with me. Dad was upset at me for getting angry. I tried to tell my father what happened.

Dad told me how wrong it was to get mad at Aunt Vanna. I tried to explain the circumstances but my father didn't listen to me.

James was upset. He asked for the phone. He stated strongly to my father that his sister had been completely disrespectful. The call ended badly.

Unfortunately, my father and I did not speak for 6 months.

And that was the last time I spoke to Aunt Vanna.

CHAPTER 4.

A TERRIBLE DEATH

There are no secrets, that time does not reveal.

—Jean Racine

"ARE YOU SITTING?" Mom asked me.

"Yes. What's going on?" I answered wondering what happened.

"Your Aunt Vanna died, and I heard she was all alone in her apartment."

"What? How do you know Mom?"

It had been twenty years since Vanna and I had argued.

"Your brother called me. It took the police an hour to get to her body. Apparently, there was a very bad case of hoarding," Mom continued.

"What? This is crazy!" I exclaimed. "Hoarding? What? Why did they call my brother?"

"The police called your brother because his name was the only one they could find in her phone book with the same last name."

"Oh good God," I moaned. "Not so great Mom. Shocking really. Maybe all that hate came back to bite her."

"Apparently it was one of the worst cases of hoarding the police have seen," Mom continued, shocked herself by the news.

I couldn't believe it. I didn't see any hoarding when I was in New York. This was all outrageous.

Mom continued to tell me that Aunt Vanna's body was badly decomposed and there was little left of my aunt from the rats and maggots. The stench was terrible. She had been dead for quite some time. Eventually, someone had called the police.

She was dead all that time and no one knew.

Aunt Vanna had alienated herself and no one in the immediate family had spoken to her since my father died six years before her. I was thinking his death might have affected her badly. Also, thirteen years before her death, 9/11 was a devastating experience for her. She had told my mother that soot came falling down on her in the park where she was sitting that day. I suppose we all remember where we were that awful day. But being a few blocks from the towers, Vanna was so close to the destruction.

I thought it was a sad end for this woman who caused so many difficulties for others. No one deserves to die like that, no matter how bad they are. Little did I know that this was just the beginning of a series of events that led to my *awakening*. I had buried the abuse for years.

We hung up and I thought back to my visit with my aunt. I was wondering what happened. Vanna had spread her *hate* to so many people, no one wanted to be around her.

It was a beautiful sunny day and I decided to go outside with my dogs, Loo and Chuch, to look at nature like I always did.

I laid down on my lounger. My thoughts drifted back to the last twenty years since Vanna and I had spoken. I was married for close to twenty years and had a son going into university. My husband and I had our own marketing business for twenty years. I had dedicated my life to rescuing animals. Life had ticked on.

There were so many years of not knowing what Vanna was doing. There were so many questions.

I was sitting peacefully listening to my waterfall, looking at the trees contemplating all the news when my phone sounded. It was my mother forwarding me an email message from Aunt Vanna's cousin. His son David, had sent his father a message. David had looked after Vanna's affairs.

David's email said he was thinking about Vanna the week before she died when he was in New York. He had driven by her place in a cab and thought he might go in. "The person she wanted all her money to go to was Noah's daughter Laura," he said.

I stared at the email. *Even after I have not spoken to her all this time? Could this be true?* I questioned. I was stunned.

My heart sank.

"She wanted her estate to come to *me?*" I whispered in sadness. I felt a tremendous amount of sorrow and started to cry. My aunt had no children or husband, and it saddened me to think she thought of me after all that time.

I started to think back to my many memories of my aunt and reminisced about her and what had happened throughout my life.

I called my mother.

"Are you kidding me? What was that message Mom?" I inquired.

"You need to go to New York and go claim what's yours," Mom demanded.

Mom had spoken to Vanna's cousin who said to tell me to get to New York right away.

"I can't do that Mom, I have no idea what's going on, I just can't jump on a plane."

"Well, I think you should go," Mom answered, trying to encourage me to get to New York.

"Maybe send that message to my brother since he is dealing with police," I suggested. I thought perhaps he should know this news since he was communicating with the authorities.

He didn't email me or phone. He was quiet.

I phoned David and talked to him. I hadn't spoken to David since I was in my early twenties. I had met him briefly with my father. My father was visiting me when I was living on my own in Toronto.

David told me that he had stopped speaking with Vanna fifteen years prior to her death. They'd had a silly argument and she wanted her will back. He had been made executor and had been given the document, but after the argument, she wanted the will returned.

That was the last anyone had seen of it.

I told David how shocked I was to hear all the news. One – how shocked I was to hear about the hoarding. And two – I couldn't believe Vanna had any estate at all. And three, I was in complete shock that Aunt Vanna would think of me as a beneficiary. Especially after our argument.

David told me that yes, she did have money, but he had no idea how much. Apparently, it was a sizable estate. I told David that my brother was involved as the police had called him first.

"What? Vanna *hated* him!" David exclaimed.

Well, Vanna hated everyone, I thought.

I asked David if he would want to look after the estate. I thought since I hadn't talked to my aunt in all these years, it might make sense for him to do it. Plus, Aunt Vanna had wanted him as executor in her will. He was happy to oblige. He was quite fond of my aunt.

I hung up the phone feeling a huge sense of relief.

***

Everything was upside down. We had a hoarder's apartment full of garbage. We had biohazards in the apartment, due to my aunt being dead for so long. (She was dead five days or more.) And, we had a body that couldn't be identified. There were no dental records, doctor's records or fingerprints. There was no will. Nothing. Not a great start.

A few days had passed and David phoned. He said that he had spoken to a lawyer who told him that being a distant relative, he could not administer the estate and it would need to be administered by the closest relatives. That meant my aunt in England, my brother and myself. We would need to apply for the administration papers. David gave us the name of the lawyer he had spoken to. We hung up the phone.

I felt so disappointed at the news. I didn't know how I was going to administer the estate with my brother. Deep down, I didn't trust him. But, I ignored my feelings and I thought maybe he would be okay. After all, Mom had told me that he had changed.

My brother and I arranged to speak to the lawyer. In our discussion, we learned that because the will was buried somewhere in that rat and maggot infested apartment, the estate would go intestate. That meant my brother would be entitled to a percentage of Aunt Vanna's estate. A percentage of who knows what, but in my brother's mind, there was money involved – for him!

A long-forgotten voice started to speak to me, *Listen to me. I have much to say*, the lost voice said. I ignored her.

After the phone call, we decided we would try and apply for the administration papers of Aunt Vanna's estate. I told my brother I would phone my Aunt in England and let her know what we were thinking.

When I phoned my aunt to tell her that we had spoken to the lawyer and were wanting to administer the estate as it was potentially quite sizable, her immediate response was one of anger. She hated her sister. Aunt Adena enlightened me on the stories of the bullying and how much of a miser her sister always was. Her memories of

Vanna coming home to Scotland and asking her poor ageing parents for money bothered her very much. Plus, Vanna was always angry at her sister for marrying her best friend's husband.

Aunt Adena told me how Vanna had also caused a huge argument years ago when my grandfather had passed away. Adena had asked Vanna and my father for a share of the money to put up a gravestone for their father. Vanna was furious. My grandfather was not a religious person, so in Vanna's opinion, she didn't think a gravestone was necessary. Vanna immediately phoned my father and, not long after, both my father and aunt phoned their little sister and swore at her. They both stopped speaking to her. Vanna had caused the worst argument that you can imagine. It was a disaster. My Aunt Adena was so sad when she told me about it. She loved her brother, my father, very much.

"It could be a million dollars; I don't want any of *her* money," Aunt Adena roared.

"But, maybe your children would like the money if there is any," I suggested.

Aunt Adena was adamant. There was *no way* that she wanted anything of *hers*. I understood. Aunt Vanna had that effect on people.

I phoned my brother. I told him it would be us looking after Aunt Vanna's affairs. Aunt Adena was not interested and wanted nothing to do with any of her sister's estate. He thought that was great, he was now entitled to half of the estate.

My brother started sharing his plans with me on how he was going to *spend* the money. He wrote that he was going to build a greenhouse. I think he wanted to sell lettuce to large grocery stores and retailers. I thought it was very unrealistic. My parents had always told me that my brother would come up with illogical business ideas. They would roll their eyes and look at me in disbelief. This was just another one that he was dreaming about that made no sense.

I thought that if there was anything in the estate, he might want to think about helping his children. I had spoken to my brother's wife who mentioned how she wanted to help their children. But those thoughts never crossed my brother's mind. I responded saying to my brother, that we had no idea if there is anything even there. It was all speculative.

I had a feeling of uneasiness that continued to nag at me, but I completely disregarded my little-forgotten voice. Something I had done for many years.

I had buried the abuse and thought it was over.

Chapter 5:

A Whispering Voice

Trauma is personal. It does not disappear if it is not validated. When it is ignored or invalidated the silent screams continue internally heard only by the one held captive. When someone enters the pain and hears the screams healing can begin.

—Daniel Bernock, *Emerging With Wings: A True Story of Lies, Pain, And The LOVE that Heals*

THIS WAS THE FIRST TIME I'd had to deal with my brother directly since my childhood. When my father died, I managed to get through his death without any incidents. But he had a will.

Dealing with Aunt Vanna's estate, I started to hear about Swiss bank accounts, platinum certificates, IRAs, multiple bank accounts. Some accounts were in White Plains, New York, where my aunt had mentioned she had some affluent friends. I learned that White Plains was a tax-free haven and that many New Yorkers conducted their banking in that town.

Many rumours were swirling about Aunt Vanna and how she was able to accumulate such wealth with secrecy. The person who helped her with finances and taxes seemed convinced that earlier in her life Vanna had a lengthy stint as an escort!

I concluded that if this was true, Vanna was not the stereotypical escort, but, perhaps, accompanied wealthy elderly gentlemen to functions.

I thought that the money she had accumulated, came from the affluent gentlemen she may have become friendly with. Perhaps they offered Aunt Vanna some very shrewd financial advice. Aunt Vanna was very intelligent, well-read and could command attention in any social setting. I could certainly imagine her at parties with socialites, not being out of place and even controlling conversations on a variety of topics.

This was my theory gleaned from discussions with a person who knew her money matters first-hand. After the Emmy Award, I had no knowledge of my aunt ever being employed again in her life. And that was decades ago.

***

We started the administration process. It was going to be a lengthy one.

My brother told me he didn't want to communicate using email, but I insisted we communicate in writing. I thought having everything in writing was essential in any situation that involved estates and lawyers.

But as communications began, my brother's emails, texts and

phone calls seemed incoherent. Convoluted. Aloof. I was getting short messages without explanations. I heard conflicting information from my brother. He was repeating inconsistent details that he had heard from other people and I was getting confused and frustrated. There seemed to be many different scenarios.

I wrote to my brother that the situation was making me feel crazy and he wasn't making sense. I told him that I only wanted to know facts.

Then, I asked my brother to try and use some discretion. My brother had mentioned the rumour we heard about to the police. I was surprised and astonished he would repeat such a thing. This was gossip and why he would repeat this to the authorities was beyond me. I said it wasn't a great idea to mention rumours to police. I asked my brother to let the lawyer handle things; let him do his due diligence and the process would take care of everything.

It was then I started to receive my brother's cryptic emails.

My brother emailed me saying I sounded very official. He then told me to stop telling him what to do. He asked me if I thought he was stupid and said he had made only one comment to the police.

"why should anything make you crazy anyways... you hated her and are lucky to be getting anything, if we get anything anyways, not that I deserve anything either, but I far from hated her and wanted a relationship, especially for my daughter..." he said.

I looked at the message. "He thinks I'm lucky to be getting anything?" I murmured under my breath. I felt my stomach go in knots. I had a sense of panic.

It was a warning sign. It was the first trigger for me.

Even though every fibre of my being was saying *stop right now*, I ignored my gut feelings. Having a lifetime of denying the truth, I learned to live with all the secrets for years. I was a good girl and was taught to deny. So I was doing what I was told.

My brother continued on about how he was only interested in

my aunt's accomplishments, her history, and not the money. He said he wished he had a better relationship with my aunt because he had learned so much about her talking to our relatives.

His email then turned ugly. "think about it Laura.....what do you really deserve ?...did you even care before david said he saw an old will."

I put my iPad down. I had a thunderbolt feeling. It shot through me. I was frantic and a little confused. I felt completely unsettled.

I took another look at what he said.

"What do I really deserve? What is that supposed to mean?" I shrieked.

My thoughts went wild, *I am the one who stayed in touch with my aunt throughout my adult life. Who is he to say what my aunt did with her money or her estate? Is he suggesting I don't deserve anything because my aunt and I had argued? What if that was what Vanna wanted? Didn't he think that was important?*

My brother's email was a red flag.

I read on. My brother told me whatever comes our way was found money. He then said that money does strange things to people and he went on to say that he had done nothing to endanger my potential inheritance.

"Wow!" I whispered to myself. I was sitting on my bed. I took a second look at what my brother said. I was in knots. I laid down on the bed and looked up at the ceiling. My thoughts were going a mile a minute.

Money does strange things to people? So he's suggesting I am greedy? I thought. There was an underlying message in his words. Yes, I was criticizing my brother on his handling of the estate, but this was another ploy. My brother's insinuations that I was greedy and that I was lucky to be getting anything were absolute lies and completely contrived.

Jitters were rampant. A long lost voice in the back of my head whispered, *Please don't trust him.* But I still didn't listen.

I had an inkling that my brother was jealous when he heard my aunt had left her estate to me and that I was the sole beneficiary. Seeing the messages I was receiving, I think it bothered him immensely. There was an enormous amount of jealousy and hate when we were children and I thought this was over a long time ago. I was discovering it wasn't so.

I went to bed and tried not to give it too much of my energy. I had become such a positive person in my life. Something I had worked very hard to do after years of child abuse and neglect.

In the morning, I took a long shower. I must've been in there for about a half an hour. I was wondering how this was all going to go with my aunt's estate. There was so much that we didn't know. I got dressed and picked up my iPad. I glanced and saw another message from my brother.

Again I was full of anxiety.

My brother told me he was very sorry. He said that his email the previous day was much stronger than he actually felt and explained it was because he was very tired. "it does feel that you have changed your attitude towards vanna, only because of the fact that she had a little money and that there was once a will naming you as a beneficiary," he wrote.

He then said he thought I was overreacting because I was so concerned about what he said to the police.

My stomach tightened. Another trigger.

Being told I was overreacting completely got my back up. For years my brother had told my parents I was overreacting to his psychological and physical abuse. He had always made light of it.

My brother then blamed the situation on bad karma because of my aunt and wanted me to have confidence in him.

The message then took another ugly turn. He said, "please just remember that you really did hate that lady and that if a will really does still exist, it is only because she was a hoarder, and not necessarily because it was her final wishes."

The hair stood up on the back of my neck.

Yes, I had argued with my aunt and disliked her very outspoken ways, but if there was a will that had named me as the beneficiary, it would be what my Aunt Vanna wanted.

I was experiencing some old buried feelings that were long forgotten. Lurking deep were some buried nightmares, and they were rising to the surface.

I completely ignored my brother's incorrect assumptions. I replied back. I reiterated my thoughts about how my brother should use some discretion when communicating with the lawyer and the police. I said it was causing confusion when he repeated what people were saying. It was all hearsay. I told him the facts would be revealed once a lawyer was involved. I wrote my brother a list of all the conflicting comments I had heard.

My brother, in no way, seemed interested in what my aunt's wishes were. The emails he had sent were not concerned with the truth.

***

I started to talk about the details of the estate with the lawyer. I was feeling overwhelmed. The costs of trying to administer Aunt Vanna's estate were going to add up and we had no idea what we were dealing with.

"Laura, this is the unknown here," he stated explaining how complicated the process was.

"There might be back taxes, hidden debts, cleaning up the apartment, surety bonds and more." The list was endless.

"You don't know what's going to happen," he warned me.

"Well, I'm not sure I can do this," I replied.

"It's a risk Laura, and I guess you're going to need to make a decision if you want to take the risk."

We hung up the phone. I needed to give it some thought.

We had only heard that there was a sizable estate, but everything was completely speculative. There were way too many unknowns.

I wasn't feeling comfortable about the whole situation. I phoned my brother and said I was out. I just couldn't do it.

I was relieved. I also felt sad and guilty, but there was so much we didn't know. I had a myriad of mixed feelings.

Being from Canada, I had no way of knowing what to do next.

I phoned the New York County Public Administrator's office. The communications were slow, and I needed to be patient as they seemed inundated.

After a lot of probing and waiting, I was finally instructed to fill out the *Report on Death* forms and have them notarized. The County's office told me that once the office received the documents, they would arrange to have their investigator go through the apartment and try and retrieve important documents – safety deposit box keys and most importantly, try and find a will.

I spoke to the administrator.

"Oh, that would be amazing," I said to her. "I feel at a loss. I'm up in Canada and can't get to New York. Maybe we can finally find out some answers."

I was hoping that the investigator would give us more information. Find out something. We were all in the dark. My aunt had been so secretive. Her hoarding was a mental illness no one knew about.

A few days passed and I got a call from Jake. He was the investigator who took the case. He was outgoing and friendly. He talked with a strong New York accent. It reminded me of being there. Jake was really helpful and I had many questions.

"According to the police, the hoarding is quite bad," I told Jake when we first talked.

"Well Laura, we see it all the time here in New York," he informed me. "Hoarding is very common because the apartments are so small. It's something I'm used to."

Jake said he would call me after he had been in the apartment.

My mind went into overdrive wondering what possibly could be in the apartment. I questioned if it could be as bad as the police said it was. It was difficult for me to get my head around it.

I watched videos on hoarding and speculated if my father's death had spiralled Vanna into a downward spin. Maybe it was 9/11. I just was perplexed by the whole situation.

***

After a few days had passed, Jake called me. Right away, I could tell by the tone of his voice he was stressed.

"Hi Laura," he said out of breath. "You have no idea how bad it is. The state of your aunt's apartment is absolutely devastating."

He was shaken. Jake tried to explain how terrible the apartment was, but he had a hard time conveying it to me. It was that grotesque.

"We even put on two masks to try and keep out the stench. The smell was so bad – there were rats and maggots everywhere! I've never seen anything like it," he expressed with an exasperated voice.

I felt bilious. I completely understood. When I had rented an apartment years ago, across the hall, a man died without anyone knowing. The smell was indescribable. And I just couldn't imagine how terrible all the rats and maggots were. Gruesome. It wasn't only the smell that was so vile. This was a horrendous case of hoarding. He said that he had not found the will or safety deposit keys and it was very difficult to find anything with the garbage piled so high.

"How could this have happened? I am still trying to figure this out."

"I don't know Laura," Jake answered, "but it is bad."

"My great-aunt Rachel was a hoarder," I added, "and the funny thing is Vanna stayed with her aunt when she first came to Canada."

"That's interesting," Jake commented.

"Listen, Laura," Jake continued, "we didn't find a will. But, I did retrieve recent bank statements that showed a large estate. I go into a lot of apartments and look after many cases. If you want my advice, I *highly* recommended that you try to look after your aunt's affairs,

You shouldn't let this go. Come to New York and take care of this. It should be easy."

"I don't know if that's possible Jake. But thank you so much," I stated. "And I really don't think it will be that easy."

We hung up.

I thought I should talk to my husband. This was a decision I needed help with.

James and I discussed the pros and the cons. We decided maybe the family should try and apply to administer the estate. If we didn't, it would be handled by the Public Administrator if we decided not to, and I heard it could take up to ten years. I didn't feel right just leaving it. James agreed.

I phoned my brother and shared what the investigator found. I told him that I thought it would be best to try and administer Aunt Vanna's estate. I said I would phone my aunt in England to let her know what we were going to do. My brother agreed. Immediately, he said to make sure I got my Aunt Adena to sign an agreement that she was out. He seemed concerned about percentages.

"Let me phone her to see. But, if she's changed her mind, in any way, we need to respect that," I informed him.

"I was only kidding," he snickered.

I winced at his *joke*. Everything was always a joke with him.

I didn't think it was funny and ignored him.

I phoned my Aunt Adena to give her the update.

"Laura, I've changed my mind. I've thought about it, and I want to help. I think you're right. If there is any money, I will take it for my children. Please let me help you," she suggested.

I contacted the lawyer.

We were all going to look after the estate.

Chapter 6.

Ignited

Just because something isn't a lie does not mean that it isn't deceptive. A liar knows that he is a liar, but one who speaks mere portions of truth in order to deceive is a craftsman of destruction.

—Criss Jami

I FELT RESTLESS. MY INSIDE VOICE, my true self, Little Laura, was trying to get me to hear her long forgotten voice, but I still wasn't listening. I had been taught to ignore my instincts and what my true feelings were telling me.

Red flags and signs were there, but I continued to ignore the uncomfortable feelings I was having. I just wanted to get through this situation and settle my aunt's estate.

Over the years, I took great pride in thinking I was such a strong woman. I had worked for a bank for over ten years. I had my own business for two decades. I had a great family with a wonderful husband and son. But every time I talked to my brother, or received a communication, I felt a physical reaction. There was an underlying fear. My blood pressure rose. My heart rate accelerated.

Something was very, very wrong.

I let my Aunt Adena and my brother know the amounts for the first instalment – the amount needed for the lawyer's retainer and court filing fees. I spoke to my aunt and emailed my brother: "Could you please send as soon as you can. Want to get this going as it may take weeks to get the papers in order. My address is below."

I really wanted to get the deposit to the lawyer because I knew by talking with him, it was going to take some time to get things sorted out.

My aunt's cheque came right away, all the way from England, arriving only days after I asked her to send it. My aunt respected my request and had posted the cheque quickly.

But my brother's emails went silent. The phone went silent.

After not hearing anything from my brother, I decided to phone him on the weekend to follow up. It was a natural thing for me to do. Being in the corporate world for decades, I had learned to micromanage everything.

We spoke. My brother said that he had family visiting. He said he was *very busy* and had little time for my phone call. I felt my uneasiness. I could almost hear my brother's snickers through the phone. He had always told me what an idiot I was when I was a child.

I spoke to my brother about getting his DNA kit together. In order for us to identify Aunt Vanna, Aunt Adena, my brother and I needed to courier our DNA kits to the New York Medical Examiner's Office.

Then I asked if he received my email with the amounts owing.

He snickered, "Yes." It was disingenuous. His voice had that tone of self-importance. He sounded insulted I would ask. I knew he was smirking at me like he always had.

I felt uptight. My body was tense.

This was *another* warning sign for me. Again, I completely ignored my body's signs. I fluffed them off.

My brother said he was going to take care of everything on Monday. I hung up the phone hoping he was telling me the truth, but there was an underlying feeling of distrust that continued to hover over me.

Monday came and I texted my brother to check he had done what he had said he would. He was to send me his cheque and send his DNA kit to New York. He texted back saying that he had done so.

After so many years of burying my past, I continued to brush aside what my true inner child was telling me. The godawful feelings I was having when I communicated with my brother.

***

I got an unexpected call from the New York Medical Examiner's office. I looked at the number coming in and suspected something was wrong.

"Hello, Laura speaking."

"Hi, Laura. It's Betty here."

I had spoken to the office so many times, we knew each other by name.

"Your brother just called me and he seems confused about sending the DNA kit," Betty informed me. "He doesn't have the courier account number."

"What do you mean Betty?" I asked. "I'm sure that my brother has already sent it."

"No, Laura. Your brother called me for the courier number. He doesn't have it on the kit." She said that she would give my brother the number and we hung up.

My brother said he had already taken care of everything to me. But he hadn't sent the DNA kit as he said. He had lied to me. Triggered again.

Sitting at my desk, I heard a little voice, Little Laura, inside me say, *Please listen to me. Don't you remember his constant lies?*

I immediately picked up the phone and called my brother. There was no answer. I got his voice mail.

"Don't you *ever* lie to me," I warned him. I remembered the rampant lies when we were kids. Lies were never ending. My brother had always made me sound crazy, denying anything I ever said.

My brother phoned me back and gave me his list of excuses on why he didn't tell me the truth.

All the warnings signs were going off like fireworks, and I continued to shun and deny them.

Work was very busy, so I put everything out of my mind. It was one of the busiest times of the year for me. My husband and I were designing event materials for the Toronto International Film Festival. The project was stressful and deadlines were tight. Owning our own marketing business together, we always needed to make sure we were available for our clients. This was a large project that needed our full attention.

Almost two weeks had passed and I had not spoken to my brother, and I received no phone calls, emails or texts from him. I really wanted to get the process going but thought I'd give my brother some time to get his cheque to me.

I eventually went to the mailbox thinking I had given plenty of time for my brother's payment to arrive. I walked home with a pile of mail in my arms. I hadn't collected our mail because I was so involved with work.

I walked into the house and dropped all the envelopes onto the kitchen table. They scattered about. I kept looking for my brother's letter amongst the mound of envelopes, but nothing was there. No cheque! I looked at my husband.

"Oh for FU*K sakes!" I shouted. James saw how upset I was and didn't say a word. I threw the mail down on the table and ran downstairs to our basement to phone my brother.

My husband stayed quiet. James knew. My inside voice, Little Laura knew. But for decades, I had kept silent. And I was doing what *good girls* should do. Stay silent. My mother's words, "Don't make waves Laura," had been ingrained in my head. That was our family way, "We shouldn't talk about it."

I phoned my brother.

"Where's my cheque?" I immediately snapped when he picked up the phone.

"What? You haven't received that yet? I told my wife to send it," he sneered. "Let me check with her to see if she mailed it."

His reply was quick and without delay. I suspected it was another lie. I felt so angry and out-of-control. The situation was unravelling. And I was seeing old behaviours. I could see the contradictions and started to feel nauseous. I had a flashback of my brother smirking at me when we were both punished for his lying about a family statue he broke.

I decided to phone my mom. Mom had always stayed out of the fights.

"My brother is doing it to me again," I grunted.

"Why? What's going on Laura?"

"My cheque isn't here and he's blaming me and his wife," I told her. "My nerves are so high."

"Don't get upset Dear," she pleaded. "You must watch your blood pressure." Mom tried to calm me down.

"I'm feeling terrible fears," I told her. "My jitters are all coming back. I'm really feeling horrible."

"Laura, don't let it get to you," my mother continued. Mom really didn't know what to say. Mom had never taken sides when I was a child. Mom's answer always was, *Just don't let it bother you.*

"I'm trying, Mom. This is all too familiar."

I hung up the phone not sure how I was going to handle this situation.

The next response popped in from my brother. I read it. I apparently *knew* how busy he was. The manipulations began!

Oh my God! I had no idea. The list of excuses started rolling in. All that was needed, was a *simple apology*. But my brother could never take responsibility for anything as a child, and here he was, doing the same thing as an adult.

As I read my brother's message, I found myself getting more and more agitated. I could feel the anxiety in the pit of my stomach. His words were like nails on a chalkboard. I was triggered in the worst way.

I wrote to my brother and asked him to e-transfer his payment. My fingers were hitting my keyboard in dread and anger. "I am not going to be waiting for payments," I told him.

I was desperately trying to keep my composure.

My brother completely ignored my request and told me that the cheque would be sent the next day. He went on to say that calling him a liar was disrespectful. I took a second to think about what he said. I had <u>asked</u> him not to lie to me. I called him no such thing. He had completely twisted what I said.

Little Laura's voice whispered to me again, *Laura, you need to listen to me. Don't you remember he called you a liar every time you told the truth?*

I left my desk.

I was feeling unsettled and out of control. This was not me. I told

James I was going for a walk. I needed to just take myself into the present moment. I didn't like what I was experiencing.

"Come on Loo, let's go," I said to my rescue dog. I couldn't wait to get out.

We crossed the street and went for a long slow walk. Loo must have sensed my feelings as she walked right next to me. I looked down at her. She looked so beautiful. She was the calmest dog I'd ever rescued. I looked at her long black fur blowing in the wind and how happy she was. She looked up at me smiling. I remembered the day we rescued her.

When we had picked her up, she sat in my arms. All ten pounds of her. A little sweet puppy with a beautiful face. By the time we got home, my coat was soaked. Loo was not very good in the car. The movement of the vehicle didn't work for her.

Loo had never attended dog training. She didn't go to "puppy socialization" or do the three levels of dog training like our other dogs. Yet, she was the most obedient and affectionate dog we'd ever had. There was a *knowing* with her. Was it that her mother came from such terrible circumstances that she carried that somewhere inside her? It was a mystery to me.

We walked down along a long trail in the forest across from our house. It was quiet. When we got to the end of the trail we entered a big open field and I sat down. There were bails of hay bundled and carefully placed by the farmer. They were all over the field and one of them invited me to sit down. Loo sat next to me.

"Oh Loo, why is this happening?" I asked her.

I had my arm around her feeling her soft fur. It always felt like black velvet to me. She looked over at me panting. I always talked to Loo because she was so intuitive and seemed to understand.

"I thought this was over long ago; this thing with my brother," I whispered to her petting her face. She kept looking at me with her big, brown eyes and kept panting. She seemed to understand every word I was saying.

We stayed and gazed out into the field and just looked around. Just the two of us. I cleared my head and tried to get rid of my negative thoughts.

I let Loo off the leash and she ran and got a stick; one of her favourite things to do. So sweet. I threw it and she ran and picked it up and brought it back to me quickly. Loo looked like a black retriever and she fetched like one too. She always ran back with anything we threw.

We played for a while and then Loo sat back down with me.

"I'm so glad you're in my life." I gave her a big hug.

We continued to sit and just watch nature for a while. After I was composed, we got up and walked back home in peace.

I felt tranquil. I was now in a better frame of mind and ready to go back to my brother's menacing email.

I walked in and went back to my computer. My brother had nonchalantly told me to be patient and not get so stressed telling me that the bills would get paid. It didn't seem like a big deal to him. I think he was trying to make me feel like I was stressed without reason. He then told me he was sure my aunt's cheque had only just arrived. However, I had her payment a few days after asking for it.

The apology didn't come. It was the "Not-My-Fault" syndrome. Something I was very familiar with. It was complete disrespect.

At the end of the email, my brother told me to take a breath. He then said it was not worth increased blood pressure, making light of his actions.

My old childhood feelings were now ignited. My brother's email left me feeling completely twisted inside.

My brother ended with love you.

Chapter 7.

A Leopard Doesn't Change its Spots

Marmite – a sandwich spread from Scotland. It is a very dark brown, sticky paste with a very strong taste – and smell. The marketing ads say, "Love it or hate it." I hate it. After eating it, your breath is foul.

It was the weekend. I was watching TV. My parents had left us alone. I was laying on my stomach on the floor, giggling and laughing at the most hilarious show on earth, Bugs Bunny. It was the best show on TV for me. At six years old, the cartoons were insanely funny. I didn't notice where my brother was and I didn't notice my brother eating his Marmite toast.

He finished. He crept over to me. I wasn't aware of his presence. He grabbed me and forced me over. He gripped my arms so I couldn't get away. He held me down. He was so much bigger and stronger than me.

I struggled to get away – my head flying side-to-side. He sat on top of me laughing. My hair was under his knee and I couldn't lift my head. He licked my face and forced his breath on me. His breath was revolting. Vile. He was laughing. "Stop!" I screamed. "Stop it!"

He pretended he was going to spit on me. Saliva dangling from his mouth. My helpless body struggled to get away. I kept screaming "Get off of me!" The more I continued to scream and struggle, the more he laughed. This was funny to him. After he felt he'd given me enough of his abusive control, he let go. He walked away smirking. Empowered.

"You're such a baby," he snickered.

To this day I can't even think of eating Marmite.

I HAD JUST WANTED HIM TO DO the right thing and pay me his share of the costs. My brother did not like that I was telling him I would not accept a cheque and that I was calling him out for his actions; asking him to take responsibility for his delaying his payment.

My mother and I spoke again. I was so disturbed by the toxic situation.

"Crap Mom, I'm so upset by all this. Are you kidding me that he's changed?" I expressed. I was mad I had believed Mom that my brother had changed his nasty ways.

Mom sighed not knowing what to say.

"I cannot believe all this bullsh**. You were way off!"

I hoped Mom would say something.

"Why don't you call his wife?" Mom suggested, "and she will set things right."

"Hmmm, maybe I will. I'll send her a message as this is getting out of control." But I was hesitant.

It was not an easy thing to do — deciding to write directly to my brother's wife about this troublesome situation. I was really nervous about doing it. All the dark secrets had been kept quiet from my brother's family. I knew I was crossing the invisible line trying to reach his wife. But, I was angry. And I wanted the truth.

I put my fears aside, and I wrote my brother's wife even though I knew I was breaking the "toxic rules".

I told my brother's wife exactly what my brother had told me. I asked her to tell me the truth and wanted her to confirm what my brother had said to me. I told her that it didn't sound like her to not send a cheque to me. She had seemed to be a very responsible person. Reliable. I said that perhaps she might want to have a discussion with my brother and said that this was to be the first cheque and the estate process might be a couple of years.

"I am not going to have my blood pressure spike like this with his lies..." I exclaimed. I told my sister-in-law that my brother was turning the situation around to make it sound like it was my fault.

Then I wrote to my brother and told him I refused to deal with him and his lies.

My brother's wife responded. I was hoping that she would have an answer for me that would make sense. Maybe I was wrong with all my triggered feelings. Maybe I was blowing this all out of proportion. Maybe I was just seeing this all wrong.

But it didn't happen.

My brother's wife completely ignored all my questions and said that my brother sent the cheque and I would receive direct payments going forward.

My questions were left unanswered.

I told James what my sister-in-law said. We were going to receive a cheque by courier. James said that was simply unacceptable and texted my brother's wife telling her that he would not accept a cheque. James' protective nature had kicked in.

My feelings of despair were coming back – all these years later. Anxieties and fears were unbridled.

I wish I could have stopped the agitated feelings that I was having, but I had no control over them. I was stunned at what was going on. It was mind games and distorted lies back in my life all these years later.

This whole situation was extremely difficult. It was only a few months before this situation with the estate, I was hospitalized three times with high blood pressure. My blood pressure rose to 259/135 on the first visit to the emergency. Normal blood pressure should be half that reading.

That day, I was feeling unwell. I couldn't put my finger on it. I looked in the mirror. My right eye was drooping. *That's weird,* I thought. Maybe it was the make-up. As the day progressed, I continued to feel terrible. James said that I had to get to the hospital.

Upon my arrival, the nurse in emergency took my blood pressure. I was immediately admitted and brought into a hospital room. It was chaotic. Doctors were concerned I might have had an aneurysm. They pulled James aside. "If that's happened, it's fifty-fifty," the doctor said. My husband couldn't believe what he heard. I was wheeled away for a CAT scan. When I came back, the doctors asked for my permission to take fluid from my spine. Analyzing the fluid would determine if I'd had an aneurysm. It was the only way to know for sure. I agreed. Thankfully, the tests were negative. The next day, I was released from the hospital.

One day later, I felt ill once again. James took me to the drugstore to take a blood pressure reading. I printed the reading. It was 244/129. My husband took it to the pharmacist. He asked if the machine was calibrated and gave the pharmacist the printout. She went white. She looked shocked.

"Go to the emergency," she insisted. "Right away!" she continued with a stressful look on her face. Once again, I was wheeled in, immediately, from the hospital emergency and doctors worked quickly to lower my blood pressure to normal levels. I was released the following day.

It was the weekend and I couldn't arrange to see my doctor. I had to wait. Unfortunately, that night, I had another episode.

I was lying in bed with my son, Mitchell, watching *Survivor* like we always did. I was looking forward to seeing it. I loved the show and had taped it. The TV went blurry. I started seeing lights. Flashing lights. I was so scared. I sat up and my son held my hand.

"Breath deeply Mom," he had said stroking my hand. He told me to just stay calm and keep breathing deeply as I had taught him. He kept stroking my hand reassuring me everything would be okay. My husband called the ambulance.

I was carried out of my home on a stretcher. The paramedics were all looking at each other in complete shock that I was still conscious. My blood pressure was through the roof. It was a miracle I was alive. It was extremely dangerous. I swear Mitchell saved my life that day.

It was a very scary time for me – until I got my blood pressure under control.

Thank heavens for James and Mitchell who were there to help.

Chapter 8.

Triggers

My husband had heard about all my childhood abuse, so he didn't like my brother. It deeply disturbed him when I told him the horrific stories of my physical and psychological abuse. When James first met my brother, he told me it was insufferable. I had fallen in love with someone who could see underneath a mask. James could see through the lies. He was determined to protect me. He told me that no one was ever going to hurt me again and said he would protect me at all costs.

When I told my husband about witnessing animal abuse as a child, it really upset him. I saw how much James deeply cared about animals. We both shared our compassion for animals and talked about having animals in our life when the time was right.

Teddy was our first dog. Our little seven-pound, white, fluffy puppy, a Golden Retriever, came to us when our son was only four. We all fell in love. Teddy was the most beautiful puppy we had ever seen. Unfortunately, bad breeding left Teddy with many health issues. We were continually at the vet.

Teddy was always so sick. He would have terrible diarrhea. Night upon night, my husband would take Teddy out to the backyard. Every hour, poor little Teddy needed to go outside. Teddy's bouts of sickness would last for days. James got little sleep, if any. Sleep didn't seem to matter to him. He was only concerned that Teddy was okay. He told me that Teddy would look up at him with his sad eyes wondering what he did wrong. It was like he was saying, "Why am I always sick? I'm just a little puppy." James felt Teddy's pain and was always there for him. It was just one of his kind-hearted acts.

Teddy was a great dog – there is a reason why people love Golden Retrievers. They love everyone and greet you like you've been away from them for years. Unfortunately, Teddy never got "healthy". But we did our best to try and make him well.

When Teddy was seven, he had been sick for a few days. Nothing we were trying was working. We had just moved to a new house and didn't have a veterinarian.

When Teddy went out to do his business, he passed an enormous amount of blood. Teddy was getting worse and we knew it was serious when we saw the blood clots. James quickly took Teddy to the car. He lifted him into the back and told me he would drive as fast as he could to get Teddy to our old vet's, two hours away. Teddy had had so many health issues over the years; my husband wanted Teddy to see the vet that was familiar with his history.

By the time James arrived at the vet Teddy couldn't move. The vet team ran out to the car and carried Teddy inside. My husband called me to say they had arrived safely. He was crying and extremely distraught. I knew how upset he was – Teddy and James had shared so many nights together, my husband's heart had Teddy's paw on it.

The news was bad. A tumour had burst and Teddy had been bleeding internally. Our vet said when that happens, there is nothing that any vet can do. Even if my husband had arrived there earlier, there was no saving Teddy.

James went in to see his best buddy. Teddy was in pain and panting. He was having a hard time breathing. My husband held him. Teddy died in his arms. He saw Teddy take his last breath.

James still cries thinking about Teddy. He can't talk about it. My husband has a heart as big as they come.

JAMES WAS GETTING MORE AND MORE furious with my brother and his refusal to see the situation he was causing. My husband was very concerned about my health and knew my brother couldn't care less.

James had written my brother the day before. His message was to the point. For many years, my husband had suppressed his anger at what my brother had done to me as a child. He had kept the peace, like the family wanted, and said nothing for decades. As long as my brother didn't cross his path, there were no issues. Now, my brother had crossed his path and James' anger had surfaced.

James's message was clear. James had told my brother that the *cheque only* method was archaic and that there were many other options for payment. My brother was concerned about getting an accounting record for his business.

James told my brother he would be issued a receipt immediately after a bank transfer. My husband expressed his extreme frustration to my brother, saying, "You operate thinking everyone's an idiot."

James then said that he handled our banking matters and he was expecting a cheque from my brother after we had sent the breakdown of payment details. He stated that my brother was to issue a payment to us at the time the expense was incurred, as he had committed to do.

"That did not mean whenever you got around to it or felt like it," he stated.

James had said that there was no way that we would "float" my brother's portion of the expenses and that the third installment had been received from my aunt – all the way from England. He then said that my brother's payment, from only a few hours north, was late and blamed on my brother's wife and her *forgetfulness*. My husband then said he would forward bank transfer information and stated to my brother that he would need to deal with him regarding finances.

"Stop upsetting your sister, I won't allow that after her recent health issue. You and your antics have her blood pressure elevated... that stops NOW! Finally I strongly encourage you to not continue with me...that's an avenue and outcome you won't appreciate," he said to my brother.

His email stated that if my brother could not handle his obligations, then he should get out. James told my brother in no uncertain terms, that we were not dealing with him again. We would only communicate with his wife.

I felt such a great sense of relief knowing that my husband could see through my brother's façade.

***

James suggested to me that we should get out for one of our special walks with the dogs. We needed to find some sanity. Everything just seemed the opposite of sanity.

Being very close to a beautiful sandy beach, we decided to hop in the car and take Loo and Chuch with us. Chuch, our Havanese, had been suffering from lung cancer and we had to be careful not to take her on really long walks. She was twelve and we called her a "silver spooner" being a purebred dog. She loved her walks but was having a hard time breathing. But she was game to get in the car and go.

Water had always had a positive effect on me, so I couldn't wait to get to the beach. The dogs were whimpering and excited to get there.

We arrived and got out of the car. The beach was incredibly calming. It was windy and the sound of the waves was deafening. The waves had large whitecaps rolling in making the most amazing, incredible sound. It was like music. Mesmerizing. In the distance, we could see the mountain where we lived. It was picturesque.

I could hear the waves thrashing themselves onto the shore. The seagulls were soaring in the air looking to find some scraps of food. Some of them were nestled on the beach soaking in the sun. The wind was strong and I could feel my hair brushing against my face. I took a deep breath and felt my tension falling away.

I took off my shoes and felt the warm sand on my feet. I felt serenity running through my body. We started to walk along the shore as Loo and Chuch were running around enjoying the freedom. There was something intoxicating about nature and animals, and sand on my feet.

I looked back and saw our footprints in the sand. I thought of a wonderful quote from Martin Luther, "Animals are footprints of God." And our animals were so important to us.

After a while, James and I talked about the unpleasant circumstances. We agreed that things were completely wrong in this whole situation. This was to be our first payment from my brother, and he couldn't meet his first financial obligation.

James and I agreed that this was probably not going to get any better, so we would need to remove ourselves from the situation if things continued like they were.

"It's too bad," I pointed out, "because the whole process should be an easy one. But my brother is making this difficult."

James took my hand and we continued to walk along the beach in solitude listening to the music of the waves. James always saw the truth. It was so great to feel so much support.

We got home and I felt relaxed from nature's calming effect.

That evening my brother wrote to me again. I saw the email come in and my stomach immediately went into knots. It seemed every time I got myself calm, I was triggered by each message that my brother sent. I would get stressed out.

My brother listed all the things that were wrong with me and my husband and stated that money wouldn't change his heart.

"I really didn't think that your husbands absolute lack of any family values would rub off on you, but I guess when you live with a hateful, spiteful person long enough, somehow you get changed...."

My brother's message ended with how much he still loved me.

What is he talking about that I have no family values? I questioned to myself. He couldn't be serious. I was looking at his email just shaking my head in disbelief at what I was reading.

I was a loving wife and mother in a twenty-one-year marriage. I had looked after my ill father for five years when he was sick. I had always been there for my mother – for every holiday, to help her move, to assist her with illness. My brother had never shown up, at any time, to help.

My thoughts were spinning around and confused, *Because my*

husband says the truth, speaks his mind and is trying to protect me from having a stroke, he is hateful and spiteful? And, James's refusal to accept a cheque after waiting two weeks for payment made him a bad person?

I, again, questioned my brother's unjustified statements. James was an easy scapegoat.

Two minutes later my brother sent another message.

He said, "... forgot to say... I am so sorry your blood pressure has spiked as high as mine."

Oh, Lord!

I felt the pressure building again. I looked again at my brothers twisted words.

Money has changed me? What money? My stomach was tight. We had no idea if there was any money at all! My brother kept mentioning the money. Everything was uncertain.

He loves me? My brother's hatred was vile as children and he was very jealous – now I could see my brother's hatred for me as adults. If he loved me, why was he saying and doing the opposite? If this was love, then I wanted no part of it.

This situation could have been avoided with a simple apology for not putting a cheque in the mail when my brother said he would. **Take responsibility for it.** That was it! It was that simple.

But there was no way my brother would do it. He simply would not apologize. And now I was alive with old buried anger.

The bank transfer didn't happen and we said we were out.

Chapter 9.

One-Thousand Words of Excuses

💬 *Rescuing a cat is not something I thought I'd ever do. Initially, I thought bringing a cat home to a house full of dogs would be a problem.*

I decided to volunteer with our local Humane Society. They asked me if I was okay with cats. I said "Sure. Why do you ask?" "We have an abandoned house with one hundred cats. And we need help." The building for the Humane Society was not quite ready and this was where they had placed the cats in the meantime. I was up for the challenge.

When I first arrived at the house, it wasn't quite what I expected. I thought maybe the cats would be in cages and I'd need to give them food and water. I wasn't prepared for what I encountered.

The minute I walked in, there was a terrible stench. Cats were running around freely, with fur flying everywhere. There were little bits of blood on the floor. Trying not to let the smell and dirt bother me, I cleaned the litter boxes as best I could and put out the food and water. I vacuumed the rugs and left.

When I got home, the smell was on my clothes and in my hair. I needed to put my clothes in the laundry and take a long shower.

I continued volunteering for a while, coming home and showering — doing what I could for the cats. Mitchell had come with me and seen the state of the house, so I suggested to James that he join me on one of my visits — to see the craziness himself.

When we first arrived, I could see the look of absolute shock on his face. I started my cleaning and he looked around in dismay. After a while, James asked me if I had seen the black cat with the long fur. I had no idea which cat he was talking about. There were so many. This cat had sat right in front of him looking up, very dignified. There were cats running all around and it was just chaotic, but this cat sat so quietly and just stared peacefully at him.

I sat down on one of the chairs and said, "I have no idea which one you are talking about." No sooner had I said that when the cat with the long fur came and sat right on my lap. "This one?" I asked. "Yup, that's the one," he replied.

That next day, little Buddy came home with us.

When Buddy arrived, he was sick. He had blood coming from his rear end and he smelled very bad. The poor little guy had been in that house for over a year. I don't know how he did it. We took Buddy to the vet to get some medication for his infection and gave him the bath he so desperately needed.

At first, we put Buddy in Mitchell's room. Our dogs were very interested but we had no idea how everyone would get along. Every day, we opened the door only a few inches, so they could all smell one another and get used to each other.

After a week, we figured it was time to let Buddy out of the room. We opened the door. Buddy waltzed out like he owned the joint. The dogs smelled him, and he just walked around without hesitation and explored our house.

Buddy had his claws but we never saw him use them. He liked to sharpen them on his cat scratcher, but he always let me clip them with my nail clippers. Buddy would purr when I touched his paws. He used his paws to touch you gently when he wanted a pet. He used his paws to hold you while he was kissing you. If you lay down with a headache he would come and place his paw on your head, where it hurt. Somehow Buddy knew. He did not have a mean bone in his body.

Just recently we lost our precious Buddy. He had a massive heart attack and died right in front of us. It was heartbreaking. We still can't talk about it. Buddy was given a second chance in life. I wasn't a cat person until we rescued our little cat, Buddy. He will be remembered forever in our hearts.

I T WAS THE LABOUR DAY LONG weekend. James and I planned to go away with Mitchell. The timing was great with all that was going on with my brother. Being self-employed, James and I rarely had taken long vacations. Weekends were our only vacations.

"Buddy you'll be okay for a few days," I assured our cat. "We won't be too long."

We felt a little guilty leaving Buddy in the house all by himself. He was such a social cat. We didn't like leaving him alone but made sure the house was full of food and water for him. Loo and Chuch were going to visit their favourite friends' house. Friends of ours, who had rescued two Golden Retrievers, were happy to have our dogs for a few days.

We travelled to a small town six hours away in Michigan state. It was nice to get away and not think about all the trouble that had been going on. The trees were starting to change colour, so it was a nice drive just looking out the window. James and I loved taking drives. It was always a good chance to clear our heads.

James and I held hands. I looked over at him and smiled. James' strength had always amazed me. James was hit by a drunk driver when he was seventeen. He was in a coma for a week. James always drove with such care when we were on the road. Mitchell listened to his music in the back seat with his headphones on. It was a beautiful scenic drive.

We arrived at the hotel and James put the suitcases down in our room. I don't know why, but I checked my iPhone. I guess it was a habit. There it was. Another message from my brother. Again, I was full of trepidation.

I glanced at it. The email was so long, I had a hard time looking at it. Trying to ask for an apology from my brother had spiralled him into a flurry of excuses. The message was confusing, littered with spelling mistakes, and it rambled on and on. No capital letters. No paragraph breaks. It was extremely hard to read.

I decided to wait to read the message when I got home. I said nothing to James. I just didn't want to talk about it or ruin our little holiday getaway.

Being in the U.S., it was a great chance to shop for some clothes and just try to escape the madness. I was so happy to find some Liz Claiborne purses on sale and a beautiful red leather jacket. Not being a big spender, James always had to encourage me to buy clothes.

After our long weekend away, I got home in a new frame of mind. We had a wonderful time. We walked in and Buddy was happy to see us. He was rubbing all over us like he always did. After we settled in, we went and picked up Loo and Chuch from our friends' house. But, I knew I was going to have to deal with *the message*. I was not looking forward to reading it. I wish I didn't have to deal with it, but I had to.

I told James my brother had written again and I was going to respond.

I went downstairs to my computer. I started to read it. I felt anxiety all over my body. I was tense.

I still had a hard time making sense of it. It looked like a bad football play to me. It was like a maze and I didn't know which direction it was going to take next. Almost a thousand words of excuses, lies and manipulations. Never ending. It must have taken hours for my brother to write the message trying to explain how right he was that he didn't send the payment.

I read the first sentence. My brother said that he wasn't mad or upset at me, "... in any way." My immediate thought was, *So, you're not mad at me because you didn't send me your cheque?* The palms of my hands started to sweat.

I didn't really want to continue to read it, but I had to even though I knew it was upsetting me.

My brother mentioned my blood pressure and told me that I should let things roll. He suggested that I should learn to meditate.

My eyebrows went up. I was confused. Since I was a young child, I had prayed and had practised meditation my whole life. My brother knew this about me.

My thoughts were whirling again, *Why on earth did he say that? Isn't he aware he is causing my elevated blood pressure?*

As I kept reading, it felt like bees were swarming around me.

My brother said he had done nothing wrong other than being stressed and not respond fast enough. His sweet talking email just got my stomach tight as a knot. Those words! I heard those words my whole childhood. My brother's relentless bullying was always coupled with, "I've done nothing wrong." The statement completely made me flinch.

I was uptight – bewildered by the first few sentences.

Just walk away! Little Laura cried to me. But something made me keep reading the long email of complete rubbish. How crazy was all this? It was just one lie after the next. But not even a lie, it was twisting of the truth which was much worse.

"Laura, you know perfectly well what we were going through the 2 weeks that you waited for me to get things done," he said.

My brother was putting words into my mouth. Sparked again. Judge Judy's words, *Don't tell me what I knew*, came flashing in my head. I rolled my eyes reading my brother's manipulative words. It was smoke and mirrors.

My brother told me it was the most stressful time in his twenty-three years of being in business.

I whispered to myself, "Man, I've been really busy at work. How long would it have taken to quickly pick up the phone or fire a few words in a text to let me know? Ten seconds? People make time for things that are important to them."

The excuses continued. He said he had no idea that I was anxiously waiting for the cheque. I was baffled. I had expressed many times to my brother how anxious I was to get his payment.

The message was a long winding unscrupulous string of words and was very difficult to read. I was only looking for one word. Sorry. But all I kept reading were excuses and twisted lies.

My brother said that his wife was away babysitting their grandchildren for four days when I called to see where my cheque was.

I stopped. I thought, *Four days? Didn't he tell me in a previous email she was away six days?* Sure enough, I checked the previous message. You have to have a good memory if you are going to be a good liar. My brother had completely forgotten what he had told me.

The email continued saying that he couldn't believe that I would think he wouldn't pay me – he didn't know where this was coming from. He said we were family and he had given me no reason to think he would never pay his fair share. He told me he wasn't a charity case either.

He didn't know where it was coming from? I thought. *Is he insinuating James is influencing me?* There was such an underhanded inference with his statement.

"A charity case?" I said out loud. "I'm just asking for a freakin' payment." I could not believe what I was reading. I felt like I was going crazy. My anger was bubbling in my whole body, along with intense anxiety.

And as I continued to read on, I continued to feel like a Mack truck hit me at one-hundred miles per hour. I looked at the palms of my hands. They were sweating again. I felt myself getting more and more frustrated by my brother's complete lack of respect.

My brother continued with a lengthy explanation of why he lied to me about sending his DNA kit.

The confusing message veered off.

"I have changed my mind about responding to james's emails, it really is not worth the aggravation and they are so "not us" for lack of a better term ..... other than pointing out that you did tell me that you were waiting for my cheque to pay the lawyer but james seems to be saying that he has paid the lawyer already and is waiting for you and I to repay him ? which is the truth ?" he asked.

There it was again! Twisting his words. James was so not *us*? I would never put myself and my brother together – in anything!

I re-read what my brother wrote about the payment. "Is James saying something to my brother that I am not aware of?" I whispered questioning my memory.

My husband and I had shared bank accounts. We did not pay individually for anything. I went and talked to James.

"Just wondering if you ever told my brother you paid the lawyer?" I asked. "He seems to think you did."

James looked at me.

"What are you talking about Laura? I said nothing of the sort," James replied.

My brother was trying to cause trouble between James and me.

I was feeling like my life was turning upside down. The one-thousand-word email continued saying that this situation should be between us.

"he put a riff between you and your father, then you and your mother, and now he is attempting to do the same with us. we are family, blood, brother and sister," my brother said about my husband.

My brother finished saying that he was sad we hadn't kept in touch all these years, and then continued, "... which has saddened me more than almost anything in my life."

My brother's email ended telling me he loved me.

Oh, my goodness.

The word "sorry" would have sufficed or simply, "I screwed up." The whole situation could have been put to bed with one word.

Fifty years later here it was again. Blame and sabotage. The Not-My-Fault syndrome. My brother's words were in plain writing and

I saw nothing had changed since we were children. As a child, my brother continually had lied to my parents saying it was me who was lying. Daily.

I sat in complete amazement. I was staring into space.

Loo came running down to the office. She sat in front of me shaking me out of my shook up state. I looked her, "What's up girl?" I asked her. She just sat looking up at me.

"Loo, you doggies make our life so sweet." She looked at me with her big brown eyes. I was petting her head feeling a little bit better, and another email popped in.

"Oh God, not again," I said to Loo. I immediately had a feeling of dread. I hesitated to open it. I knew it would not be good.

Against better judgment, I opened it anyway.

My brother's first line in the message suggested that my emails were being screened by my husband because I hadn't responded to him for a few days.

Oh goodness! "My husband was screening my emails? Really?" I whispered in frustration.

I had shown James nothing. That was not something I would ever do. I considered my brother and my communications as being between my brother and myself. In addition, James was an eye-for-an-eye type person. He was old school. If he had seen the emails, I knew his protective nature would have kicked in and he would have lost his temper. He was already fed up with my brother and his lack of concern with my health issues when my blood pressure rose to dangerous levels. Plus, he was aware of all my buried secrets of horrific child abuse.

I responded to my brother and explained I was away on a mini-vacation. I stayed as professional and calm as I could. Thirty years working in a corporate environment, I learned to write clearly with thousands of messages to clients.

I told him that he still was blaming me for him not sending me his payment.

No apology came. My brother still could not understand that he was still pushing the responsibility onto me for him not putting the cheque in the mail. I apparently knew very well how busy he was.

My brother wrote me that he gave up. He said he had no clue what I was blaming him for. Then, in the next sentence, he said to me again that I knew what was going on with his deadlines. He apparently told me how busy he was every time he texted or called.

Every statement was deceitful.

I had to take a second look again at what my brother wrote. I was blaming him? I never said I was blaming him. What I was doing was asking him for a simple apology and to take responsibility for his actions. My brother was blaming me, saying I knew he was so busy. He had also blamed his wife when I first asked where the cheque was. Who was blaming who?

Every time he texted or called? I had no communication with my brother for almost two weeks.

His words. They were tricky.

My brother had blamed me for his wrongdoing. My mother was very wrong. He had not changed. I had believed her.

He was still just as poisonous as when we were kids.

Chapter 10.

The Assassination

Be certain that he who has betrayed thee once will betray thee again.

—Johann Caspar Lavater

A FEW DAYS HAD PASSED AND THINGS had settled down. Thank God.

I started to investigate the costs of clearing out my aunt's apartment. It was just sitting there with all that garbage, and it needed to be cleaned up.

I contacted a few companies that specialized in cleaning up biohazard waste from hoarding. I learned that it was a specialized process and the prices were incredibly high. One of the companies took photographs of the apartment. They sent them to me. They were grisly. Hard to look at.

It was simply devastating. I wondered if this could this be the same apartment I was in only twenty years ago? I could not believe how grim the hoarding was. The company said the hoarding was a Level Four. The only thing that elevates hoarding from a Level Four to a Level Five is if there were carcasses of animals. Thank heavens my aunt did not have animals.

Pictures showed garbage bags and paper piled everywhere, from wall to wall. I was not sure how my aunt got in and out of the space. There must have been tunnels.

The living room had paper and garbage bags piled four feet high. There was a large framed picture of the Gorbals sitting on top of all the garbage. Her bedroom had the bed turned sideways and clothes were thrown everywhere. My aunt's little black travelling bag that she had used when she came to my apartment was lying amongst the clothes. Underneath the rubble were remnants of her past life. Books still on the bookcase seemed untouched in years. My aunt's record collection was still visible. From what I saw in the pictures, she was still listening to her Billie Holiday and many jazz records. There was a life underneath all that garbage. A life that went terribly wrong. It was dreadful. It was very difficult to even think about those pictures. My aunt was very mentally ill. Hoarding was a devastating illness we knew nothing about.

I thought about what the landlord had said, that in Vanna's later years, my poor aunt was rummaging through dumpsters and picking out the garbage. So sad. I saw no signs of hoarding when I was in her apartment.

I started investigating my aunt's will. If there was anything I had learned with regard to estate matters, it was incredibly important to get a will professionally written by a lawyer.

I had some questions on my mind. I decided to contact David to see if he had ever spoken to my aunt about her will. I asked him if he knew if it might have been written with a lawyer or if it was simply a homemade kit. I suspected it would have been written without a lawyer. My aunt was such a miser, I guessed she wouldn't have wanted to spend any of her money on a lawyer and have her will notarized. I had learned that in New York State, handwritten wills were not valid.

David answered me stating that the will was handwritten. I then asked if it was ever notarized. David answered again saying he thought it wasn't, but he couldn't remember for sure.

My conclusion was that my aunt had died with an invalid, holographic will and it was too bad. I thought David had done her a great disservice not knowing the law, or advising her to get her will written with a lawyer.

***

After a few days passed, my brother emailed. Every time I saw his name, I was triggered by negative emotions. I was completely vexed he wouldn't leave me alone.

My brother stated that he *just heard from* the lawyer and the lawyer informed him I had decided to back out. My brother said he was going to *take it up from here.* He said he would inform my aunt in England and talk to the lawyer the next day regarding next steps. As always, he signed off on how much he loved me.

My anger had peaked.

I was getting more and more irked at every communication. The bent and distorted words from my brother were setting me off.

He just heard from the lawyer? I thought. *He is doing it again for crying out loud.*

I was miffed. Why not state the simple truth and say he contacted the lawyer? My brother had said he had *just heard from* the lawyer who we had *first spoken to* about Aunt Vanna's estate.

When I started communicating with the *first* lawyer on moving ahead with getting the administration process started, he had put me in touch with his partner who was more specialized in looking after estate matters.

Why would the *first* lawyer contact my brother out of the blue? It made absolutely no sense. My brother made it sound like the *first* lawyer had *just* contacted him.

Bloody sneaky.

I was infuriated. My brother had such a grandiose self-image, he was refusing to understand that with a criminal past and drug history, it was extremely unlikely he could administer in the United States. My brother had been caught drug trafficking in his late teens and convicted. He was also a former drug addict.

In addition, both my Aunt Adena and I were just not comfortable with him administering the estate. We felt he was untrustworthy and highly incapable. My aunt had told me she preferred I administer her sister's estate. She also remembered my brother as a child. She had an enormous fear of mice. My brother pretended to have a mouse in his hands and had put his hands on my Aunt Adena. He scared her. It was funny to him and not funny to her. That memory stuck with her.

My brother's email ignited me. Again. I couldn't contain myself. This had gone on long enough. I could not tolerate it anymore. I fired back. There was no way an untrustworthy person was going to administer this estate.

I replied immediately. Anger was running through my veins.

I told my brother that I assumed *he* had contacted the lawyer. I asked him how he was going to come up with the money. There might be expenses for the biohazard cleanup, renovations of the apartment, a surety bond, a retainer for the lawyer and escalating subsequent lawyer's fees.

My brother had worked sporadically. I had always heard how much he was struggling with the business. It was beyond me how he thought he could pay for these enormous expenses. Plus, with his many lies and excuses for delaying payment to me for our first retainer to the lawyer, he had shown his complete inability to meet financial obligations.

I shared the information on Level 4 hoarding and sent him the pictures I had received of my aunt's apartment. I told him about the possible expenses.

I said I had learned David had helped my aunt write a handwritten will, which wasn't valid in New York. I then shared my confidential thoughts, "... It was nothing resembling a Will. He did her a big disservice... She died thinking she had a Will."

I'm not sure why I decided to share my intimate thoughts with my brother on how frustrated I was with David's handling Aunt Vanna's affairs. I knew it was a big no-no.

Maybe it was a test. I sensed my brother would contact David and share my private email with him. I suspected he would talk badly about me and distort what had happened. I also suspected a smear campaign of me had started right away when my brother first started communicating with David.

Remember how he would tell everyone I was making things up? Little Laura's voice asked me. My Little Laura's voice was finally being heard. I was watching patterns of behaviour that were the same as my childhood.

I left my computer and went and found James.

"Want to take the bikes to the water?" I suggested. "This whole thing with my brother is driving me nuts."

James said it was a good idea and we went and got our bikes. Living in a resort town, we loved escaping to the trails for some stress relief.

We decided to ride to a park that had a little cove that was beside the water.

James road ahead of me and I peddled behind. Our ride was easy and slow and I just enjoyed the wind blowing in my hair. I could stay in the present moment when I was doing something outside.

I felt I was peddling away from all that trouble.

We arrived and parked our bikes and sat on the bench beside the water.

I walked down to the bay and took off my shoes. I stepped into the clear water and looked at all the stones. I was always careful when I walked in the water. It always needed to be clear.

I looked at the scar on my shin and thought back to when I was living on Prestwood Road when I was ten. I had taken my bike to the river at the end of the street. Kids were jumping in the river and wanted me to jump in. I really didn't want to, knowing how many bloodsuckers were in there.

As the kids continued to tease me, I gave into their taunting and jumped in. When I came out I looked down and there was a black bloodsucker on my shin. I panicked. I drove my bike home crying and screaming. I had arrived home and Dad was outside. I showed my father my bloodsucker, completely feeling like I was going to die.

Dad came over. He started laughing at me. He grabbed the bloodsucker and pulled at it. It eventually came off and my leg was bleeding badly. Blood was running down my shin.

"It's nothing, Laura," he said laughing at my reaction. I ran in and took a Kleenex and wiped my shin.

I felt my body tight at the memory.

I looked over at James. I felt appreciative I had someone in my life that always validated my childhood pain. Someone who had such a strong sense of right and wrong.

We rode home and that night I went to bed forgetting all about the manipulations of my brother.

***

The following day it started all over again. David emailed me.

There it was – *the assassination.* My suspicions were absolutely right! David wrote me just one day after I had sent the email to my brother.

I recognized my brother causing trouble right away. It was the same sabotaging behaviour that I had experienced as a child. My brother never respected my boundaries.

Remember when he couldn't wait to make me cry and then he'd laugh at me? Little Laura reminded me.

I was upset.

David told me that my brother had called him. He said my brother was *kind enough* to share with him some comments I had written in my email. David wanted to clarify he never wrote the will or advised my aunt on how to make a will. He wanted to clarify he had never been schooled in New York law. He said *he had done no one a disservice and found that accusation or insinuation, rather insulting.*

My brother was deliberately causing trouble. What a distressing thing for him to do.

My brother was kind enough? I thought. My brother probably spoke with his sweet voice while he was stabbing me in the back. Kind was not the first word that I thought of when I remembered my brother's cruelty to me years ago. My brother's bullying was mean-spirited.

David was a distant cousin and had not been in touch with our family growing up. He had no idea what my brother was capable of. David had only heard from my Aunt Vanna how much she hated my brother, but I don't think David could have possibly known my brother was trying to cause trouble.

This was the final blow. That was it. I lost it! I was furious. I wrote my brother to stop emailing! This was over. I was done.

My brother failed his test. And now he had proved to me he was just as mean as an adult.

Chapter 11.

War

It's silent. Underneath the water. I can hear nothing. It's very peaceful. I was in complete shock from what I had just seen. I had run into the lake across the street from where I witnessed it — another violent act that I was completely devastated from. At eight years old, I had seen and witnessed many acts of cruelty to animals. But this one completely over-whelmed me.

We had moved to a house on a dead-end street—Prest-wood Road. It was much bigger than the last house we had. It had an extra bedroom, a dining room and a room set up for the kids to play in. I loved this house.

The house had a forest for a backyard. Across the street was a beautiful lake that I often swam in. I was a good swimmer. The YMCA had asked my mother if I could join the swim team. She said no, telling me that the chlorine would bother me. I really wanted to be on that swim team, but there was nothing I could do.

Often by myself, I would go and swim. And I would also go wandering on my own to the end of the street where there was a park. The park was where a lot of the kids would hang out. I was a loner, and I spent a lot of time on my own, watching frogs. They were so beautiful to me. They were everywhere. I enjoyed seeing them hop around. They were so innocent. So cute.

It was a beautiful day. The sun was shining brilliantly. A warm and inviting summer day. I was just coming home from the park and I walked unsuspectingly into the backyard. Standing there was my brother with one of my mother's cooking pots sitting on our picnic table. It was full of water. My brother was standing over the pot with a knife in his hand. His other hand was holding some kind of skin. There were little pieces of skin on the picnic table. "What are you doing?" I asked, not knowing what he was up to. I walked up to the pot and I looked inside. There was a floating frog. It had parts of its skin missing. I could see the white of its muscles. Horrible. It was just floating there. Helpless. It was looking up at me. Oh good God. It was alive! "I'm skinning it while it's alive and letting it go afterwards to see if it lives," my brother said with an amused smile. I was so upset. Completely heartbroken.

I had seen my brother kill frogs by cutting their heads off with the family hedge shears, but skinning a live frog was even more vicious. I'm not sure if he did this to the frog to hurt me because I loved them so much. I guess it didn't matter. That poor frog was tortured.

MY STRESS SYMPTOMS, ONCE AGAIN, were high. I wanted my brother to leave me alone. I went upstairs to lay down on my bed and started listening to some Zen music. It always put me into a calm state of mind. The dogs ran up with me; happy to console me when I was feeling stressed.

My iPad sounded. I looked. It was another message from my brother. Asking my brother to *stop* and respect my request to leave me alone, had meant nothing.

I felt so upset. My brother completely ignored what I had asked and fired back his message right away. He couldn't control himself.

I couldn't bring myself to read the email. My blood pressure was elevated.

My husband came up to our bedroom to see how I was doing.

James looked at me. I was deep breathing trying to calm myself. James was compelled to step in again. He was getting more and more concerned about my health.

He wrote my sister-in-law. He told her that I had requested that my brother stop contacting me. He was mad.

Immediately, my brother responded to my husband. He wouldn't stop.

"you might have sleazed an apology from my father and sleazed another from my mother but your psychotic behavior neither scares or phases me in any way.... bring it on you hero," my brother wrote.

Oh my God! Psychotic behaviour? Because James was trying to protect me and refused to be conned, he had psychotic behaviour? My husband was the most pragmatic and solid person I had ever known. He had based his whole life on truth and fact. My brother found his scapegoat in my husband's very assertive nature. Again.

WAR!

My brother's message provoked James. My husband flipped out! He was furious! He went for the jugular! He fired his message back to my brother.

" Glad you responded you burnout ***********
coward.

To be clear, I want nothing from you...never have. I
don't associate with people of your ilk! In fact I've never
wanted anything to do with you – PERIOD! Your edu-
cated, unreasonable, bizarre wondering fantasy world
isn't exactly appealing to me or for anyone to listen to.

You should have tried to be a brother to Laura - your
entire life. Now I out rank you as her husband...I will
protect her from you and your fu** ups at all cost. No
more lies (which has been fairly consistent throughout
this nonsense), no more bullsh** (which is customary for
anyone dealing with you) no more hallucinatory thought
sequences (ie grow lettuce!!)."

James's message continued on. He wanted to be extremely clear with
him. He said to *stop* sending his messages!!! James told my brother
that he was guessing his wife may have become accustomed to my
brother's bullsh**. He then said he was wondering if she knew my
brother's behaviour had denigrated to the lowest form of douchebag –
an outright troublemaker! His message continued,

" ... The comments you shared with your cousin
were made to you in confidence, but as I mentioned in
an earlier message you have no capability for discretion,
and just another clear example of your lack or respect for
your sister."

James's email was strong. He went on to tell my brother that his
unprofessional handling of the estate was staggering. James warned
my brother to stay away from him. He said if my brother wanted a
war, he lives for war.

Then my husband apologized to my brother's wife " ...I apologize
to you personally, I don't think you have any idea the stress your
husband has placed on Laura and by extension me/us."

James's email ended with a P.S., " For the record...I have no idea what you're talking about with your mom/dad apologies. I guess when you have nothing to bomb me with you lie ?? That too pretty consistent. Coward."

My husband. A tough fighter. A fierce protector. A ferocious warrior. Someone who has a strong sense of right and wrong. James detests bullies. He will call out anyone when he sees injustice being done. And with my brother, he did just that.

Emails went quiet.

Chapter 12.

The Teapot Boils Over

A lie that is half-truth is the darkest of all lies.

—Alfred Lord Tennyson

THAT NIGHT, I CALMED MYSELF DOWN from all the insanity and stress my brother had caused. I listened to my meditation music and got my blood pressure to normal levels. I woke up in a better frame of mind. I took my blood pressure and it was normal again.

I went and made my morning cup of coffee. James was still sleeping. The dogs came downstairs with me and I let them outside to do their business. They were always my link to the sane world.

I let the dogs in and finished making my coffee.

I thought, *Do I go and read what he wrote?*

Because I had calmed down, I had the courage to read my brother's email. I went down to my desk and sat at my computer. I had no idea what he wrote but I was calm enough to look at it. I opened it.

I read the message and thought it was best to walk away. I decided to go and make myself a cup of tea. The message had upset my stomach. I plugged in the teapot. As I waited for the water to boil, I looked outside and pondered my brother's first line in his email.

He said I am mean? I was perplexed. For heaven's sake, I was anything but mean.

My whole life had been about service and helping others. I had rescued animals and volunteered with a dog rescue organization, helping abused animals, for years. I could never hurt anyone or anything. Yet, my brother was the meanest person around when we were kids. He loved seeing me cry and would laugh at me when he saw me in anguish.

I just shook my head at the twisted comments.

The teapot started to whistle. I poured the boiling water into my cup and started to stir the tea bag.

I thought again about my brother's next line. *He said that I told him there wasn't a will?* I had to think back.

"I never said that," I murmured. I *never* said there wasn't a will! Not *ever*. I had told my brother in a previous email, that if the will was found, it would be what my aunt wanted. It's important we have our last wish fulfilled. Just because my aunt was a hoarder, did not mean her will would be invalid like my brother had said. That is crazy thinking. I am not sure how my brother came to the conclusion that he did.

I made my tea and went outside and sat on my deck. The dogs came outside and were laying with me.

I listened to my waterfall. James had built it himself – a large water feature with multiple levels with a massive sound. When I kept complaining about the noise of the traffic, James decided to build it for me. I listened to the water tumbling down onto the rocks.

I looked at my bird feeder. I saw some baby birds fluttering around. Sparrows. The mother bird was feeding one of her babies. It was weird how the mother bird was so much smaller than her baby bird. It was so sweet to me. Mother Nature had been a wonderful teacher to me.

My thoughts drifted again to my brother's email, *He said he had only called David to clarify things?*

He had called David, alright, but my brother skipped the part that he shared my confidential thoughts and hurt both me and David. I can only imagine that whatever he said to David was skewed. I don't like hurting people. Being so sensitive, I always tried to avoid that as much as I could. My brother was playing sneaky mind games. He was twisting and manipulating the truth.

I looked back at the bird feeder. I sipped my tea slowly trying not to get upset again at my brother's manipulations.

I could see the family of sparrows. There was another baby sparrow that was perched on the fence waiting for his turn. I could see how nature was working in perfect order.

Once again, I thought of my brother's email, *He said that I had accused him of many untruths? Where did that come from?"*

I had told my brother to try and be discrete and not repeat what others were saying. There was *no untruth* to me saying that. Also, I had *asked* my brother not to lie to me when he was caught lying about sending the DNA package. And, all I wanted from the beginning was for my brother to take responsibility for not putting a cheque in the mail like he said he would. I just wanted honesty.

It was no wonder I had to come upstairs to make a cup of tea to calm myself down after what I read. Once again, every line, one after the next, was completely false.

The rest of my brother's email was completely menacing. He once again insinuated my husband was screening my emails and I only cared about money.

I went inside and put my tea down. I decided it was time to write my brother. I felt compelled to defend myself. My brother's mind games may have worked when I was a child but I knew who I was. A truth-seeker. A giving person. Kind-hearted. Selfless. He couldn't fool me.

After years of staying quiet as a good girl should, I thought it was time to stand up to my childhood bully and defend myself after what he had said. I knew it wasn't going to make a difference to my brother, but it was going to make a difference to me.

"Come on guys," I said to my dogs. "Let's go downstairs."

I went to my computer. I took slow breaths and calmly wrote my message,

> **❝** I just read your message you sent (after I asked you to stop) and this will be my final response to you.
>
> Yes, this is sad indeed.
>
> By all means ask David about the Will, but you repeated a confidential statement to YOU alone. You caused trouble. Now you're a trouble maker to me. You cross the line when you divulge personal comments. I know you'll never get that. But that is improper behaviour and you were just trying to stir things up.
>
> And somehow that's my fault... oh and James's too somehow.
>
> What you will never see, is you have shown a side that I thought ended when we were kids. You treated me pretty badly then. All the way back to violently rocking me in the crib... I think you hated me. Now, I don't think that's changed. Maybe a deep seated resentment towards me some how. Karma? Possibly. Just showing itself differently now. It's the same but different.
>
> You've shown me nothing but disrespect. Unbelievable. Maybe when I was young I took it, not now. Not ever.

You were a bully picking on your little sister - and now, I won't let you EVER disrespect me or lie to me.

You know... I told Dad before he died, whatever you and my brother have (resentment) let it go, and have some peace... I tried to do the right thing. Even when your daughter was not speaking with you, I told her to forgive you and move on. I have always tried to make things right.

For you to tell me I changed because of money, is offensive. You state I somehow lied to you when you have done nothing but be dishonest to me, is really nuts. I also found out that the landlord told James, you told him not to phone me because Vanna and I hated one another? What was the reason for that?

You blamed me... because you waited 2 weeks to get me a cheque (first cheque to boot) when you told me on the weekend you'd take care of everything on Monday? I guess my statement in the email, get this to me as quick as possible meant nothing to you. That is disrespectful! And that's somehow my fault. You are absolutely out of your mind.

Let me be perfectly clear — there was a Will. It was apparently HAND-WRITTEN, according to David last week — and that type of Will is absolutely INVALID in the state of NY. I NEVER lied to you. You see, I'm not a liar. I tell the truth. That's all I ever asked of you. But, you have done nothing but point everywhere else but yourself. It's James's fault, my fault... somebody else's fault. Never your fault.

Do not respond. And do not respond to James. I am strongly suggesting... you to stay away from him. You told James yesterday he has so much hate... No, he has great disdain for you.

Get some freaking help! You have deep resentments ... obviously.

No longer am I speaking with you on this matter. EVER!"

By the end of my message, I felt my heart beating a mile a minute. It was pounding out of my chest. I quickly blocked my brother's email. My hands were shaking from fear.

I walked upstairs and James had woken up and was sitting in the living room. He looked over at me. He knew right away I was upset once again. I told James what happened.

Minutes later, my phone sounded. Texts started to fly in. Blocking my brother from my email didn't stop him.

My forehead started sweating. My hands started shaking. I was having a hard time breathing.

James looked at me. He had had enough. It was too much for him. He was pushed too far. He snapped!

James lost it and phoned my brother. My brother didn't answer the phone and James got his voicemail. My husband screamed and threatened my brother. I had to try and calm my husband down from getting in the car to find my brother. The only thing that saved my brother that day is that he was several hours away by car.

I decided to call the police. Of course, the police couldn't reach my brother. What a cowardly thing to do. He completely ignored their calls to his home. How does *anyone* ignore the police when they call? No respect for the law. So, I was compelled to phone my mother. Mom phoned my brother. She demanded that he stop.

Interesting – he picked up the phone right away for my mother!

When the police finally got hold of him, it was the next day. My brother was on the golf course. The whole thing upset him so much, he was golfing.

Chapter 13.

My Awakening

When I see a bird that walks like a duck and swims like a duck and quacks like a duck, I call that bird a duck.

—James Whitcomb Riley

E VERYTHING FINALLY CALMED DOWN.
James and I giggled at the insanity of it all. James had me crying from laughter at how stupid it all seemed. We went to work and we were still talking about how everything had blown up. James looked over to me.

"Man, your brother is some kind of fu*k up. What an asshole.

I think he's a **********. He wouldn't have lasted two seconds where I come from. How the hell did you get through living with this clown?"

We laughed and shook our heads.

I was sitting at my computer. Just for interest's sake, I did some Google searches on people with abusive behaviours who think nothing of inflicting pain on others.

A video popped up on YouTube. "These people don't care about you," the psychologist explained. "They only care about themselves. *These people* have not developed a conscience."

Shock! Lightbulb! Answers! Oh, the wonderful thing called the internet!

I had a revelation. I concluded I might be dealing with something much more than just bad behaviour. There may be much more to this drama than my brother just being a creep. There might be something more than I had ever thought.

It was a fluke, but it all started to make sense. I finally started to put everything together. All these years I had been fooled and had been lied to. My mother had told me for decades that my brother had had an experience and found God. He was a changed man.

I believed Mom. And I believed my brother. Yet, I saw the same behaviour that I experienced as a child. The lies. The manipulation. The deceit. The blame. The sabotage.

Oh God, I have been manipulated. I have been a puppet. My brother did not change, I admitted to myself. *How naive of me.*

My brother's insidious and cruel behaviour had started when we were kids, but now I could see how it might have manifested into something alarming.

I started to research; hundreds of links and websites.

I read about people who perpetrate psychological abuse. I had now remembered the extreme physical, mental and psychological abuse that I suffered as a child. I realized that anyone who could torture a live animal and have no empathy about the act was extremely sick.

I saw parallels to what I was reading. The similarities were uncanny. My brother's habitual lying, manipulation and deceitfulness, no remorse, superficial charm, twisting of truth, lack of empathy, grandiose self image, taking no responsibility for his actions, no guilt, blaming me for his wrongdoing, acting without forethought not considering his consequences, unrealistic goals, and inability to control his impulses were all similar to what I was researching.

There were a pattern and history with all these terrible personality traits. They had all started in my childhood: continuous lies; lack of empathy; bullying; cruel treatment to animals; and cruelty, to me, his sister. No remorse and manipulation were my everyday norm.

And then there was the unique ability to always show people a nice face. The one I never got to see. It always seemed so fake to me. So callous. So forced. It wasn't from the heart. It was always on the surface. There were parallels to the childhood mental disorder I read about.

I learned and discovered if children with these destructive behaviours were not given treatment, there was a high risk of developing a dreadful mental disorder as adults. There was a link.

I had an awakening. I woke up after a long sleep.

***

For the first time in my life, I had a clear understanding of my childhood. I had thought my childhood was over. But I discovered, it wasn't.

I left the office. I decided to go and look through some old photographs. I wanted to look at them with a different perspective.

There were boxes of images. Quick moments of my past long ago. I rummaged through the enormous boxes looking with different eyes.

I found a picture of when I was a one-year-old. Both my brother and I were sitting on a bed of rocks. I could see a rock in my brother's hand and his arm was in the air. He was about to hit me. I was not sure who took that picture but was amazed that it was caught on camera.

Geezus, who took that picture? I thought. *Why wasn't there a mad dash to stop what I am seeing in this photograph? Where are my parents?*

There were other pictures that were very telling.

I looked at a photograph of my brother screaming at me while I was leaning over trying to see one of the toys he was given at Christmas. There was a look of innocence on my face, wanting to see my brother's new toy. The picture was snapped while he was yelling at me as I was leaning over to see what he got from Santa.

How could my parents just take pictures while my brother was bullying me right in front of them? What were they thinking?

There was another picture with my brother looking straight at the camera with his arms dangling straight down. I was beside him smiling with a lollipop in my hands. Next to me was my brother with the most threatening look of hate on his face. His eyes are squinted and his lips were pursed.

Oh yes, I remember that dark look and those dreadful threats.

I thought of that night at Christmas with the perfume bottle. I curled up my legs and tried to sleep next to a *bomb*, trying not to move. I never told my parents about that terrible night and held it in for years. I was afraid I'd be killed, just like my brother threatened he'd do.

I had to abide by his rules *or else*. I never dared to *ever* touch his things. I always felt my life was at risk. There was a deep fear he was going to do *something* to me. I was afraid to go into his room. All my brother ever had to do was look at me and squint his eyes and a surge of fear would run through my body. And I had to live with him. I had no choice.

Intimidation. Mental torture. It was mind control. I started to conclude that dealing with my brother over my Aunt Vanna's estate, had put my nervous system right back to my childhood state of constant fear and terror.

As a child, I would get so angry, but the only thing I felt I could do was grit my teeth.

"Crap, maybe that's why my tooth cracked and chipped when I went to the dentist a few years ago," I whispered looking through the pictures. The domineering and controlling of me started early. And my brother took delight in it.

I started to think about how I was always trying to defend myself. The complaints of bullying were ignored or trivialized. I was always trying to get my parents to understand what I was going through. But, unfortunately, I was met with emotional neglect.

"Boys will be boys," I'd hear when my parents witnessed my brother bullying me.

My brother never seemed to have empathy or remorse. The odd time he was punished, the discipline would not make a difference. My brother would look at the date or time and say, 'Okay, the time is up for my punishment,' and go back to being abusive. There was never any guilt for anything he did. The punishment didn't seem to work.

My brother used my vivid imagination against me. He would manipulate my mother telling her I was such a liar because of it.

Yes, it was true. I did have a magnificent imagination. It was how I kept myself happy. My imagination was my great escape because I had nothing else. I imagined myself as a teacher, a singer, an actress and a horse trainer. I would imagine myself all grown up with long hair and lots of makeup.

I lived constantly in an imaginary world where I could be away from reality. It was my friend. I think it was one of the things that got me through all the traumatic years of bullying. I continually played with my dolls and made up all sorts of scenarios. Barbie and Ken were perfect. I used to imagine they had a perfect life. I wanted my life to be just like theirs.

And somehow, through all the family dysfunction, I had faith.

I looked at pictures of that little girl with her hands together in prayer. I remembered how I was so spiritual. Always praying. I wasn't praying for God to take away my abusive brother, but always thanking God for all my blessings. I had a picture of Jesus I prayed to. I loved his picture and I talked to him constantly. Or God. I wasn't choosy. One of them was going to hear me.

As I kept looking through the old photos. I tried to find a photograph of when I was two and had broken my leg. I didn't see any of pictures of me in my cast. I wondered why there wasn't one image of me. I wondered if it was kept a secret. I wondered if it was a secret, then why?

I had learned what had happened from my mother when we had taken a trip to visit her sister in London in my late twenties.

"You were only two and you were *attacked* by a German Shepherd," Mom had explained. "You came home black and blue."

The story was told to me like I was the child down the street. I sensed my mother's detachment from it.

I had always had a vague memory of seeing white coats; being held down on a table with many people restraining me. It wasn't until I was in my late twenties when I was on that vacation with my mother that I heard about what happened.

My aunt had a German Shepherd and I commented on how I didn't like the breed. Looking at the dog scared me.

"What happened Mom?" I had asked her.

"Your brother and you came home from playing outside. You were screaming and crying. You were livid and out of control."

"Oh really?" I wanted to know more about the incident.

"When I asked your brother what had happened, he told me that you were *attacked* by a German Shepherd."

Unfortunately, being a late talker, I couldn't tell the truth of what happened, so whatever my brother said was believed. This was one of my problems. A mother who always thought her son was wonderful and believed every word my brother said. His manipulation of my mother had started very early.

"I put you into your crib and when you woke up the next morning, I took you out and put you down to walk," Mom had continued, "Your leg went the opposite way."

I was rushed to the hospital. It took four doctors to hold me down she said. My leg was broken in many places.

I pondered the story. I remembered white coats and how the doctors couldn't control me. I was kicking and screaming.

Looking back I thought about it. No dog scratches. No dog bites. No markings on my little two-year-old body that would indicate any kind of *dog attack* from the strong jaws of an 85-pound German Shepherd. I thought back to my son at two years old. If he had been *attacked* by a German Shepherd, I don't think he would have survived.

I picked up my iPad and investigated some videos. I looked at numerous movies of children that had been *attacked* by a German Shepherd. They had bite marks and stitches. It was quite graphic. And the children in the videos were much older than a small little child of two years old.

But, my brother was a good liar. A very good fabricator. He could lie without a flinch. I had questions flying in my head. How could my mother believe this complete lie? Where were the questions? Why was I not brought to a doctor? Why didn't anyone go and look for the dog that *attacked* me?

The memory I had of the event was cloudy. I remembered a German Shepherd barking. I could only think that the rest was too painful to remember. On rainy nights, I reflected on how I still held my leg from the aches. Damp weather had always reminded me of the buried abuse.

My terrifying and horrific childhood, that I chose to forget and bury, was coming back. The extreme trauma that my body was feeling, every time I spoke to my brother about Aunt Vanna's estate, was finally being heard. Little Laura was alive.

For years my abuse was lying hidden, and now my memories had come back into my consciousness. I remembered.

There has been so much emphasis on *family* in our society. Well, looking back, sometimes family is the best thing that can happen to you and sometimes family is the worst thing that can happen to you.

Chapter 14.

Back to the Beginning;
The Survival Years

I woke up. My dream had given me the answer that I had asked when I went to bed. It was a strong dream: I was travelling on a bus looking out the window. I was not noticing what was going on. I was completely oblivious. There was shuffling going on beside me, but I wasn't looking. When I looked over, there were two children fighting. One child was full of blood. I had asked God about my buried child abuse.

DAD WAS DARK AND HANDSOME WITH a big smile full of white teeth. You could see him coming a mile away with his dark olive skin and big beautiful smile. He was very charismatic. Being a salesman his whole life, that worked great for him. Dad really loved all people, so selling came easy to him. Non-judgmental, he never had a negative thing to say about anyone.

Mom was quite a beautiful woman in her younger years. Growing up in London, England, Mom trained her whole life as a professional singer and pianist. Mom had won many awards at singing competitions and was deemed the next big, upcoming star by the newspapers. She was destined for greatness, or so her mother thought and hoped. That was what Mom's mother wanted, but Mom didn't care. She didn't sing because she loved it – it was forced on her.

Mom was touring with her singing group when she met my father. The group was on the road, touring the U.K. When my parents met, they immediately fell in love. Pictures look like the movies. There are many photographs of them gazing into each other's eyes. They looked so in love.

My grandmothers on both sides were not very pleased with this newfound romance. Religion was the biggest issue. My mother's mom thought my dad was not good enough for her daughter. And also, he was Jewish. Mom was a Christian – Church of England. Dad's mother was not approving of the relationship either, because Mom wasn't Jewish.

Despite what their parents thought, my parents rebelled and got married. My father's mother refused to come to the wedding and did not attend the church ceremony.

Not long after my parents were married, my mother's mom died of a sudden heart attack. It devastated my mom. She was so young. Only nineteen. My grandmother had sheltered Mom her whole life. She had always protected my mother from my mother's abusive, alcoholic father. My grandfather had won medals for being a war hero in World War II – however, I think the war affected him badly. He had physically abused Mom's brothers and sisters, and my grandmother had threatened my grandfather to never lay a hand on my mom. My grandmother had lost two children to illness before my mother was born and she refused to let anything happen to her child.

My grandmother's overprotection may have been good in one sense, but bad in another. Mom had a very difficult time dealing with *any* issues when they arose. They were never addressed. Left alone. Avoided.

One year later, my brother was born. He was the apple of my parents' eyes – and my grandparents' too. My father's mom forgave him for getting married in a church, and she fell in love with her grandson. He had the sweetest look on his face all the time. He looked like my mother's side of the family. Angelic. Pictures show him as a happy child. Everyone seemed so thrilled and welcomed the new addition to the family.

It was Scotland and times were tough. Both my parents needed to work. Dad was the perfect salesman and Mom started a job working for Singer as a seamstress. Mom had given up her singing career when my parents were married.

With their need for a babysitter, it was decided that my dad's mother and stepfather, my grandparents, would look after the new baby. The new baby would live with them during the week and come home on weekends.

My brother was spoiled immensely. My grandparents took him away on holidays and gave him everything he wanted. With all that bonding going on with my grandparents, there was not much bonding and attachment going on with my parents. There were always two sets of rules. One set at my grandparents', and another set when my brother came home. Inconsistent nurturing. Confusing to say the least.

Intentions may have been good, but the results were not.

Three years passed, then I was born. My father was thrilled he had a little girl. He sang all the way home from the hospital. But this new addition to the family was not so great for my brother. He had to come home permanently and did not like all the attention on the new baby, me.

That's when the trouble began.

The abuse started right away. My mother started to catch my brother violently rocking my crib. He obviously had no love for his younger sister, only resentment and jealousy. From day one, he set out to hurt me.

This violent behaviour should have been a warning sign for my parents. But there were little consequences for my brother's cruel behaviour. Complete denial. There was no recognition that this could be the start of *something more* than a young child's jealousy of a newborn coming home.

My parents' conclusion was always that it was *just sibling rivalry*.

That's all.

TORONTO

When we moved to Toronto from Glasgow, I was five years old. I was introverted and shy. It went unnoticed. My extreme shyness was considered *normal*. We were a family struggling to make it in a new country. Immigrants. My parents were hoping for a better life in Canada. They had both grown up during World War II. Times had been tough.

Dad was rarely home; an absentee father. When Dad wasn't on the road with his sales job, he spent his spare time with friends. He wasn't interested in spending time with me or my brother. He loved his golf, hunting, fishing and outdoor activities. I would always hear Dad was a "man's man". I'm really not sure why he wanted to have children.

Mother was complicated. A follower. She never had a voice. She did what both my father and brother said. If there was a totem pole showing the pecking order in our family, I think both Mom and I were on the bottom somewhere. But I was underneath Mom. Really on the bottom.

I don't remember Mom ever giving me a big hug. Maybe it was because my brother couldn't hug or didn't want affection. He always pushed everyone away. I think Mom always thought if she showed any attention to me, my brother would be jealous. He had always used that and manipulated my mother saying, "You love her so much more than me." They were his favourite words to her. Or maybe it was because Mom just didn't like kids. She always said she liked teenagers much better than children.

I often wondered why Mom was so sad when we immigrated to Canada. I never saw her laugh. She always looked nice though. She looked beautiful to me. She dressed in beautiful clothes. It was always important to look nice. Mom would wear lots of makeup. Her skin was smooth, pale and flawless; fair skin against her red hair that she dyed every week. She wore dark cat-like glasses. Mom was thin and all her clothes looked so nice on her. I was a chubby kid and always felt fat. I always heard how *chubby* I was. And Mom always told me my brother was so much smarter than me. He never had to study for his tests in school. I had to study for hours.

Mom always made sure I looked perfect. She would dress me in such pretty outfits. She made all my clothes with her sewing machine. Mom would put my hair up in buns, ponytails and pigtails. I use to cry when she did my hair. My head was very sensitive.

I always had knots in my hair and Mom would brush them out. She sang to me when I cried from the pain, "There was a little girl, who had a little curl, right in the middle of her forehead. When she was good, she was very, very good. And when she was bad she was horrid."

I guess I was being "bad" by crying with my sore head.

To the outside world, our family looked *normal.* There were no signs of abuse. There was nothing that was *showing* – visually. So, to anyone who was looking, all was well.

But all wasn't well. Quiet, yes. But *not well*. Our house was a house of silence. Silent abuse. No screaming. No arguing. No items were thrown. Emotionless. My parents never argued. They never hugged either. They never kissed. The conversation was always shallow. It was a cold place; emotionally.

I knew the rules.

There was the first and main rule; never upset Mother. It was Rule #1. And a **big** rule. When there was a disagreement, Mom's way of dealing with it was the silent treatment. When there were issues, they were not dealt with. Avoid and deny. It wasn't the right way to deal with issues, but it was Mom's only way to deal with them. I learned early never to upset my mother.

Then there were the other rules.

There was Rule #2: Never get mad at either my mother or father. Honour thy parents. I always heard, "Children should be seen and not heard." It was very wrong to be mad at a parent. That was frowned upon.

And then there was Rule #3: Never raise your voice. Good girls don't raise their voices. I could never express my feelings and talk about anything that was happening. I learned to stuff everything down. So, painfully shy, I was always told what a good girl I was. I never challenged my parents on anything. I kept nice and quiet as *everyone* wanted.

There was Rule #4: Be home and on time for supper and eat all of your meal. There once was a war.

And finally, Rule #5: As long as I had no cuts or bruises from my brother's bullying, then everything was okay. And, with all that hate, my brother wanted to hurt me. Hurt me without bruising me. He knew the rules too.

***

Dad came home from work. He had on one his new ties, a white dress shirt and fancy dress pants. I ran up to him with excitement. He picked me up and gave me a big hug. Thank God Dad loved to cuddle. I got lots of hugs from my dad. He was the one I could always depend on to give me a hug.

"How's my little Dollface?" Dad asked smiling.

"Great. I am going to read in front of everyone at the next school assembly," I chimed.

"That's my girl."

I could read and write. We had just moved to Toronto. Children in the U.K. entered school much earlier than they did in Canada. When I was in Kindergarten, my teacher was very proud of my reading and writing skills. She wanted me to read in front of the school assembly and prove to the principal how advanced I was – she wanted me to skip a grade.

"She'll never be as smart as I am," my brother snickered from the living room. He was sitting in front of the TV. He never liked any attention on me. No one said anything.

The day of the reading was a stressful day for me, a shy five-year-old girl. I guess my teacher had full confidence in me. She thought that I could read my book to a large crowd of people. But the event didn't go as planned.

"Now Laura, you just walk to the middle of the stage and don't be afraid," my teacher instructed. "You just hold your book in front of you and read the words. It's easy."

"Alright, but I'm a wee bit scared," I mumbled.

I was fearful. The children always made fun of my Scottish accent, so that made me even more nervous.

"You will be perfectly fine," she assured me. "Don't you worry, there is nothing to be afraid of."

I walked on stage with my hair in a bun wearing a red and black checkered dress with my black shiny shoes. The only sound in the auditorium were my shoes clicking as I walked to the centre of the stage. Click, click, click. I stood and looked out at the crowd of people. The lights were shining down on me. I looked at my book. I couldn't read. I was completely frozen.

I looked out again into the audience. I saw my dad sitting in the second row. Dad was a big laugher. He loved making me laugh. He loved jokes and loved laughing.

I started to laugh. He started to laugh. I laughed louder and so did Dad. A minute later the whole auditorium was laughing. I kept laughing and laughing. My teacher walked on stage and helped me walk off. She was mortified.

I didn't skip up to Grade 1.

OAK STREET

Just a year after we had arrived in Toronto, we moved to a small town up in northern Ontario. We lived on Oak Street. Dad got a new job as a travelling salesman for the furniture company. I was sad leaving my only friend Nadia. But, our townhouse was much bigger than the apartment that we moved from. And we could just run out and play wherever we wanted.

From a very young age, my brother and I were often left alone together with little or no adult supervision. We had complete freedom and we were allowed to do anything. Most times, there were never any witnesses to my brother's cruel behaviour. He would always wait until we were alone.

We had independence. And free access to the cookies. I was always grabbing cookies whenever I wanted. I loved my cookies.

One day, I was in the living room sitting cross-legged on the floor. I was eating a cookie that I had just snuck from the kitchen. I loved the shortbread cookies with the red jelly in the middle. Yum. They had two pieces with white icing separating them. I would open them up and eat each piece separately.

First, I scraped off the icing from the top part and ate it slowly, licking the sweet icing and relishing in the sugary taste. I saved the jelly. Next, I ate the top of cookie with the designs on it. The jelly was next.

"TICKLE TORTURE!" my brother screamed.

He held me down.

I struggled to get away.

"Stop!"

"Tickle torture," he laughed. He held down both my arms with his one hand above my head. I struggled to get away.

He had his other arm free. He tickled me. I shrieked! I was laughing but screaming.

"STOP IT!" I cried and struggled to break free.

He kept going. He enjoyed dominating me. I was feeling crushed. I was laughing but desperately wanted him to stop.

"NO! Stop!" I kept begging him.

"Say I'm the greatest," he said laughing at me.

"NO! STOP!"

I was choking and had a hard time breathing.

He kept tickling me, laughing, "Just say it then I'll stop!"

"NO, GET OFF OF ME!"

The tickling felt like an eternity. I wrestled. I squirmed. I tried to get away. He was holding part of my hair. I was stuck. There was no getting away.

Finally, I gave up.

"Okay! Okay! You're the greatest," I yelped.

"Told you I was," he snickered, like I was a fool.

He let go and he walked away shaking his head at me like he always did.

I was so mad. I was gritting my teeth.

Mom came home.

"Mom, he was holding me down again tickling me," I complained.

"Oh, God, I was _only_ tickling her!" my brother cackled. "What a baby she is."

"I am _not_ a baby."

"Yes, you are," he said laughing and chuckling at me.

"No, I'm _not_. MOM!"

"Just stop it," Mom said to my brother.

He chucked. "Why do you always take _her_ side? It was funny. She was laughing. It was a joke."

"Just stop this nonsense. The _two_ of you."

What? The two of us?!?!

We were always lumped together. The bully and the victim.

I was always hoping Mom was strong enough to give my brother _tough love_. Maybe Mom felt guilty for not being there for his first three years. My mother refused to get mad at my brother. Instead of giving him the real-life _harsh_ consequences he so desperately needed to correct his bullying behaviour, there were always excuses.

Mom had no idea how to discipline my brother with his cunning ways. He was crafty. Most of the time, the bullying was completely dismissed and ignored. When Dad would hear about any the fighting going on, he would laugh it off. He never wanted to deal with the problems.

On Oak Street, there were three-row houses facing one another. We lived in the end unit and we faced a row house across the driveway. It was very close to our home.

One day there was a huge commotion at the row house directly across from us. Everyone was running around not knowing what to do. People were in a panic.

"What's going on Mom?" I asked Mom as she was looking out the kitchen window.

I took the kitchen chair over to the window. The window was

above the kitchen sink and I couldn't see what was going on. I stepped on the chair and looked out.

"Someone poisoned the dog. It died."

She told me that *someone* had put antifreeze in the dog's water. There were no garages and most of the containers for car supplies were kept outside. The townhouse had the dog tied up outside most of the time. His water bowl was always outside of their door.

My brother was nowhere around. I felt really terrible. Sick.

"Oh no! Poor doggie. A bad prank I guess?"

She said nothing. There was no reply. Mom never wanted to talk about anything. I think she was still feeling unhappy.

Pranks were big in our house. And this was a prank that went way beyond what a prank was. I suspected who did this wicked act. But, of course, the typical abuser will only strike when he knows he is not being watched.

I *never* saw him do it. But I suspected *he* did it.

CAMPVILLE AVENUE

A year later we moved to another house; Campville Avenue. It was in a completely different neighbourhood. I, once again, lost the few friends that I had made. As we continued to move, I continued to become more and more introverted. I was feeling so isolated. No one noticed or cared.

I really didn't like our new house. There were no children my age on the street. I did make one friend though. Right next door there was a girl who was 5 years older than me. We became close friends. My mother was very worried about me being friends with a girl who was much older than I was. It didn't seem to bother me.

That year, Aunt Vanna came to visit us. She came with her friend, Dina. I was told Dina was a singer. An entertainer. I was so awkward. I was in awe of my aunt's friend. She was very pretty with long brown hair. I wanted to grow up and be a singer just like Dina. I dressed up in little outfits pretending to be on stage in front of thousands of people. My imagination was wild with visions of being in the limelight.

Our new school was about a mile away. My brother and I would walk to school together. I would've preferred to walk on my own but Mom insisted he walk with me. My brother would walk ahead of me and I would follow. My brother never wanted to be seen with me. I always felt his anger towards me. As the years were passing, my brother's hate for me was growing more and more. And his bullying was getting worse.

"Will you hurry up Laura," my brother yelled at me. "You are such a spaz. You're so dumb."

"I am not," I yelled back at him. "Stop it!"

"Ha, ha, ha," he laughed. "See? What did I tell you? You *are* a spaz."

I looked at my brother. His words always hurt. I was sad he hated me so much.

The schoolyard separated the boys and the girls. We were separated by a big twenty-foot criss-cross see-through fence. One day after school, Jamie, a boy I had a crush on, ran over to the girls' side of the schoolyard and handed me a note.

"What's this?" I questioned to him. I was a little excited. He was paying attention to me.

"Your brother gave me this," he said and ran off quickly.

I opened it not knowing what he could have possibly meant.

The handwritten note said, "I have a crush on you. I really like you. Do you like me? Yes. No." No was circled. I was hurt, humiliated and devastated. I started to cry.

I cried the whole way home. My brother took delight in seeing me cry. All he could do was laugh. He was holding his stomach because he was laughing so hard. The more I cried, the more he laughed. He looked so proud of himself that he had hurt me so much.

We arrived home and Dad had just parked the car in the driveway. He saw me crying and distraught.

"What's wrong Dollface?" he asked.

I could hardly talk through my tears and told my father what happened. I handed my Dad the lined piece of paper with my brother's handwriting.

Dad read it and then started laughing. Somehow my father thought that it was funny! I knew Dad was a huge prankster when he was young.

"It was just a joke Dad," my brother said as he laughed with my father.

"Oh, come on now. Stop crying," Dad laughed, trying to make light of it. "Laura, it's a joke," he said trying to convince me my brother's bullying was funny.

I felt awful. A joke?!?

"You're too sensitive Laura," Dad said trying to console me.

My brother and my father continued to laugh at me.

Dad thought the bullying and abuse I was getting was no big deal. The bullying was made light of. Inconsequential. I had no physical signs of abuse. So, everything was okay.

I had no idea how my brother knew I had a crush on Jamie. I never told anyone. I did have a diary that I wrote everything in.

***

Pranks were hurtful. And unfortunately, I was always the one who was on the receiving end of the pranks being so trusting. I believed everything anyone told me.

"Do you think she'll notice?" my brother whispered to my Dad. They were in the kitchen. I was in the living room watching TV.

"No," Dad whispered. "She won't have a clue."

I pretended not to hear them.

My brother came out to the living room and handed me a glass of *milk*.

I knew they were up to something. I smelled the glass. It was filled with sour milk. It was all clumpy and had a vile smell.

"No way," I said pushing it away.

My brother and Dad started laughing. I was a target of pranks and *jokes*. They were not funny to me.

Sadly, Dad was always missing. Just gone. Never home. I wasn't sure if it was because my parents had a bad marriage, or if it was because Dad didn't want to be with my brother and me. But his absence was felt. When my brother was crying on the floor because my father had gone on a fishing trip with all the other fathers and their sons, I thought maybe my brother would learn to stop causing trouble. Dad hadn't taken my brother on the trip.

Mom was trying to console him. From my brother's point of view, he was always the victim because my dad wasn't home. In his mind, he was cheated in his childhood because Dad didn't spend time with him. Well, I was the child of an absentee father too, but I wasn't lying continually, being a bully, hurting animals and doing despicable acts like my brother was.

It was very unfortunate that my mother supported my brother's point of view and believed that her son was a victim of my father's absence. The blame went onto my absentee father for my brother being out of control. I understood why my dad didn't take him. My brother always had such terrible behaviour. There were no happy times; just problems. All the time.

Not only did my mother blame my father for my brother misbehaving because Dad wasn't around, but the finger was also pointed at my grandparents. They were often blamed for my brother's bad behaviour. I heard that it must be because my brother was spoiled by my grandparents that he was such a troublemaker.

There was a lot of blame going around. It was always everyone else's fault, never my brother's or my parent's. And as the blame went around, the bullying was ignored. It was going on right in front of my parents and it was considered *normal*.

PRESTWOOD ROAD

One year later we moved to Prestwood Road. Another move. Again. I was eight years old. I had to say goodbye to another friend – my older girlfriend next door. I was always losing friends.

We lived on Prestwood Road for five years. A lot happened on Prestwood.

Our house was a little bigger than Campville Avenue. It had green siding. Across the street was a lake. This was the best thing that could have happened to me. I loved the water. Behind our house was a large forest. Nature was everywhere. Kids were everywhere.

Summers were days of swimming in the lake and winters were time for snow angels and ice fishing. On occasion, Dad would spend time with us. In the winter we would go ice fishing; Dad, me and my brother. Dad loved ski-dooing and taught me to drive a ski-doo at a very young age.

One time I went ice fishing with Dad on my own. I didn't enjoy the fishing part but I did love being with Dad and enjoyed any time he spent with me.

A snowstorm had unsuspectingly rolled in. We packed up quickly.

"Hold on Doll," Dad yelled to me as we were heading into the storm. "Everything's going to be alright."

I held tight. It was bad.

Dad kept yelling to me that we'd be okay. I had no idea that Dad didn't know how to get back to the mainland with the snow flying in so badly. He never let me know that we were in a dangerous situation. I held on tight and eventually we made it back home. I was never scared. Dad was following the wind and the way the snow was blowing. He was very scared himself, but he never let me know.

I loved my room on Prestwood Road. My room was beautiful. I had a single bed with little flowers on my white bedspread. My bedspread had pretty white lace hanging on the edges. I was given a chalkboard to hang on my wall. Now I could really pretend to be a teacher.

My brother and I were allowed to choose our own wallpaper. My bedroom wallpaper was pink and green with lots of flowers. My brother chose black wallpaper and had psychedelic posters. His room didn't have a window that allowed any light in. The window looked onto another room in the house. His personality was dark and his room was too.

One day, my mother asked both my brother and me to come into her bedroom.

"Do you see anything wrong with this statue?" Mom asked. I knew by the tone of her voice there was something wrong.

I looked at it. I had no idea what she was talking about. It was a beautiful statue. It was very tall with a family all hugging together. It represented a family I think my mother had deeply wanted.

"No," I answered.

"Look closer."

I looked. I still couldn't see anything. My brother said nothing.

"The statue is broken and all glued up," my mother said trying to be stern.

I looked again. Looking closer, I could see all little bits of white glue hidden in the cracks. Right away my brother pointed at me.

"She did it!" my brother screamed with such conviction.

I looked at him in complete surprise. In disbelief.

"No! No, I didn't!" I ranted.

"What????? I swear to God, Mom, I didn't do it! She is lying! You have to believe me. I'm telling you the truth!" he said convincingly.

"I did not!" I screamed, defending myself to my brother's lies.

"I can't tell which one of you is lying," my mother fumed, "so you're both grounded."

I looked at her in complete disbelief.

That was a pivotal moment for me. I decided right then and there, I was on my own!

***

Mom became more absent. She was trying to find herself with her new friends who were wrestling with some mental health issues. Her best friend struggled with depression and another friend had tried to commit suicide. Mom and her friends always thought prayer would fix all of life's problems. I felt like all of us, the children, were seen as a nuisance.

I don't know if my brother was getting worse and worse, or if it was me remembering the abuse, he was almost a teenager and his actions were getting more and more defiant. Especially with the cruelty to animals.

Just like getting pleasure from hurting me, my brother got pleasure out of seeing animals suffer. The frogs. The snakes. The birds. The animals. All victims of his cruel, unhealthy mind.

It was amazing to me that my parents allowed my brother to own a BB gun. There were many times he disappeared into the forest in the backyard. God only knows what he was doing.

One day I took a walk to the park. I was on my own. I enjoyed being by myself. I saw my brother with one of his friends. They were giggling and laughing. My brother was holding a frog. He was dangling it in the air holding one of the frog's legs. I walked closer to see what was going on.

My brother had captured a snake and pinned it down at the end of its body with a rock. He was holding the frog in front of the snake. The snake was struggling to get the frog.

"Ha, ha, ha," my brother laughed. "Look at him trying to get the frog."

The snake was squirming high to try and capture the frog.

Seeing the snake tormented and seeing the frog struggle to get away, was entertainment to his unwholesome mind. I shook my head and walked away in disbelief.

But the frogs got it the worst. Maybe because they were so easy to catch. I'd shudder when I saw my brother cutting the frogs' heads off with the family hedge shears. He'd slice them off with one clean chop. Their bodies would be jumping around while their heads lay beside them. It made my stomach turn. Such a senseless death. The driveway was always full of dead frogs.

It wasn't only the hedge shears, there were the firecrackers too. The firecrackers that were meant for childhood fun, were great explosives to blow up the frogs. My brother would place firecrackers in their mouths and they would go off and the frog would be blown up into pieces. Those poor frogs.

My brother would laugh and think it was funny.

When we took a trip to Ottawa with Mom and her best friend, I was excited to go. Mom's best friend brought her daughters, Lynne and Sandra. Dad was not with us. We were visiting a new friend of Mom. The family lived on a farm.

All the kids slept in the barn in our sleeping bags. In the morning my brother woke up with a pigeon beside him. It was dead.

When we woke up we asked where the dead pigeon came from. My brother said that he had become friends with it the night before and he had rolled over it while sleeping.

I told my mother about it. But nothing happened. There were no questions. There was no inquiry. No consequences. Why wasn't there a full-blown investigation?

My brother knew how to fool my mother with his deceptions.

Chapter 15.

Getting Help

When Mitchell was born, he came into the world very peacefully. He never cried. The doctor placed him on my stomach right away and I spoke his name. He couldn't see, but he looked up at me when I called him. After twenty-four hours, we brought him home from the hospital.

I had once read how important the first five years of a child's life are, and both my husband and I wanted to make sure that Mitchell felt secure and loved. The first five years of my life were filled with terror and I was determined to fill my little child up with love and security.

The playroom was our magical place. It was filled with toys and games. His life was filled with imagination. Toys. Books. Disney movies. Oh, the numerous games we played, the stories and the puppets. Living in the land of pretending was quite easy for me.

111

There were the magic potions. Secret ingredients were put into the blender and mixed together. "Magic potion, make Mitchell invisible," I said in a deep voice. Then Mitchell would drink the magic potion. My husband and I would run around the house looking for him. He would be screaming with laughter. What fun.

There were many puppets. There was Stephanie who had a big attitude; Bird who would not say anything, but just grab whatever was in sight; old Grandpa; Kermie the Frog; Moe the Monkey; Elmo; and my son's favourite, George. I had bought George, a very expensive puppet with big brown eyes and curly hair. George was always on my hand and I made up this cute little goofy voice for him. George would come to bed with us and we would talk about the wonder of life and how magical it was. At night, we would read stories and play soft music. It was a land of incredible joy and wonder. I loved it. And so did Mitchell.

Sometimes, when we went to bed, I would make up "Peter" stories. Peter was an imaginary child the same age as my son who would need to make important choices in life. Sometimes Peter would be lost in the forest and wondering what to do. Then Peter would listen to his inside voice and find his way out of the forest. The stories were always with a happy ending, with positive undertones. I wish I had recorded those special nights, as I think the stories would have made a great book.

When Mitchell would start to drift off to sleep, I would stroke his head and tell him what a good and kind person he was and that he would grow up to be successful, no matter what he chose to do in life.

All the pain and suffering I experienced in my childhood was healed by giving Mitchell the complete op-

posite. I'm sure it was very therapeutic for me. And seeing James spend so much time with our son was amazing to me. He didn't disappear as my father did. I wish I could package those days up.

Mitchell is now in university. Over the years, my husband and I have heard what a great son we have. We are very proud of him.

NOT SURPRISINGLY, nightmares started to become quite a common occurrence for me. I was waking up in the middle of the night in a state of dread. My brother's constant threats were leaving me distressed. The nightmares were similar to the little girl who sat in front of the TV in *Poltergeist*. The TV screen is blank with the fuzzy screen. She lays her hand on the TV and turns around and looks straight at the camera. It was a similar scene in my nightmares.

I felt like a big boulder was sitting on top of a piece of paper. The boulder could not be held by a piece of paper and was about to fall.

I could never seem to explain it to my mom. I couldn't describe what it was. Just a feeling of dread. It was so terrifying. The nightmares were beyond my comprehension.

I was alone. I felt unsafe. I had nowhere to go. No one to turn to. No one listening. So where does a little girl go when she has a constant threat lurking and no protection?

In my closet. It was my safe place. It was a small closet with a wooden box at the bottom. I covered the wooden box with blankets and put my pillow in. It was dark. It was comfortable. I was safe. It felt so much better than in my room where I felt exposed. I would sleep in my closet, free from danger. My nightmares stopped when I was in the closet. Small spaces helped me feel secure. I could feel safe.

I was completely shutting down. But as a little child, I didn't know it. I was only trying to feel secure.

I needed protection. But it wasn't there.

***

At nine years old, I started taking piano lessons. My piano teacher Lydia, a friend of the family, could see that I had some severe mental issues. I was extremely introverted, had a difficult time talking and was not able to make friends. My self-confidence was non-existent.

My piano teacher was smart enough to know something was going on. She was the first, and the only person, who questioned what was wrong with me.

"What's going on Laura?" she asked.

I shook my head.

"Laura, you can trust me," she said in her very deep voice.

I was traumatized. I refused.

Lydia asked me to talk about what was bothering me. I kept refusing to answer. She kept pleading for me to tell, and I kept shaking my head in intense fear. "No, I can't tell," I trembled.

I was terrified that something really bad was going to happen to me.

Lydia eventually earned my trust, and I finally told her that my brother would do something terrible to me if I ever told about anything he was doing.

"He threatens me and really scares me," I told Lydia. "I think he's going to kill me," I gulped with my voice shaking. I was scared to death.

It was then that Lydia talked to my mother.

"You have to do something to help this poor girl, or you are going to lose your daughter." Then Lydia warned, "Laura is shutting down and if you don't do something now, it will get much worse."

Our family friend was trying to save me.

Thank God my mother listened to Lydia.

My piano teacher guided my mother on what needed to happen, and they started conspiring to catch my brother, in all his continuous lies.

That was scary for me. I had a hard time trusting my mother as she had ignored the abuse for so long. Mother had believed the ridiculous stories when my brother would lie.

"What if he finds out what you are doing?" I said to Mom terrified of my death. We were whispering outside my brother's bedroom. He was laying in bed and had on his headphones.

"Don't worry Laura. He will never find out what we are doing," she assured me.

But I had a surge of fear running through my body. The whole situation frightened me. I was re-traumatized by my mother's solution to *fix* my problems.

"But I'm so scared. What if he hurts me?"

My mother grabbed my arm.

"Do you see the bruises, Laura? Sticks and stones will break your bones, but words will never hurt you," she said whispering making sure my brother didn't hear her. "He can't hurt you."

I kept being reassured that I would not be hurt. My brother never did find out that Lydia and Mom were trying to catch him in the act. But I knew. And it scared the heck out of me.

My mother was also instructed by my piano teacher to make me go outside to meet friends. It was not something I wanted to do. Make friends? I didn't want to talk to anybody.

I cried at the door and begged to come inside. I didn't want to make friends. But, eventually, I had to venture out to meet the kids in our neighbourhood.

***

After I got some help, my metamorphosis began. It wasn't easy.

I made friends. Sadly, I was getting bullied by them. Maybe children can tell you are a target. They called me names; *big lips* or *fatty-fatty two by four*. I was an outcast in school.

One time the kids locked me in a shed.

"Hey Laura, come and see this great bike we have in the shed," they said. I walked in the shed and they slammed the door shut and locked it.

They were walking around the shed waiting for me to scream to get out. But I just sat down and waited until they unlocked the door. Eventually, I think they realized they couldn't keep bullying me. This type of bullying was no big deal to me after I had my safety threatened for years.

It was in the middle of the summer and the family was sitting in the TV room when I heard a dog yelp. It wasn't a small yelp; it seemed to go on for a long time. I didn't know what was going on. I ran into the kitchen, and Casey, our dog, was in my mother's arms. She was full of blood. She had been hit by a car.

I couldn't contain myself. I started screaming at the top of my lungs. I had no idea how to handle what I saw.

We rushed poor Casey to the vet. She went into surgery. We didn't think she would survive the accident.

Casey came through the surgeries, but she needed constant supervision.

"Why don't you look after Casey?" Mom asked. "It will be good for you and you will learn to take care of others."

It was summertime, and being a kid, it was my favourite time of year. I volunteered. I sat in the house and looked after Casey that summer. I nursed her back to health. Every day I applied Vitamin E to her torn up neck that had a very large sore. Within six weeks it was almost gone. Casey and I became great friends, and she introduced me to helping animals when they're in dire straits.

***

My personality started to change.

Grade six was the year of blossoming for me. I started to find more confidence in myself.

Two seats across from me sat a boy. He was always alone. I saw myself in him. Brian would write the same way I did. His letters were all jagged from tension in his hands. He had a bump on his middle finger, just like I did. My hand was so tense when writing; my finger had a large bump on it.

I had taught myself to relax my hand when I wrote and wanted to help Brian do the same thing. I went over to him and held his hand and told him to relax. I guided his hand so he didn't write with so much tension. His letters started to get smoother. I guided Brian, every day, to help him write better.

That same year, the principal picked me to be a captain for a school ringette team. I was so shocked. I was not in any way athletic but was thrilled just the same.

As the captain, I chose my team. There was a very heavy set girl. Her name was Lorraine. I felt bad for her. Kids were always making fun of her weight just like they did to me a few years prior. I couldn't wait to choose Lorraine. Lorraine told me she wanted to be our goalie. It was a great idea. We won the championship that year because of Lorraine. She was amazing.

At graduation, they called my name. I won the *Miss Congeniality* trophy. My helping others didn't go unnoticed. My life was getting better.

Unfortunately, my brother continued with his lack of empathy and lies. That was very clear when I was playing with Lynne, one of my friends. We were outside playing one of our make-believe games. One of our favourite games was playing horsey. Lynne was two years older than me. She was very athletic and had a love of horses just like I did. We often went horseback riding together.

We were outside pretending to ride our horses. Jumping around. Just being kids.

"Let's pretend you fall off a horse, and I will pick you up and throw you over my shoulder," Lynne suggested. "It will be just like in the movies," she said.

It sounded like a good idea at the time.

I pretended to fall off the horse, just like we planned. Lynne tried to lift me, but I was too heavy. Unfortunately, she landed right on top of me. I was in extreme pain. It was excruciating. I lay there moaning and crying. I couldn't move. Lynne ran to get help. My parents, as usual, were nowhere. She ran next door to alert our neighbour, a nurse. Lynne was frantic. The mosquitoes were crawling on me and biting my legs. I couldn't move to get them. I knew I had broken something.

Lying in agony, my brother came casually walking along, hands in his pockets. He asked what I was doing. When I told him what happened and how much pain I was in, he started laughing and snickering.

"You're such an idiot." He casually walked off without a thought leaving me to lie in the dirt.

I had broken my collarbone.

Chapter 16.

The Farm

Everyone is like a butterfly, they start out ugly and awkward and then morph into beautiful graceful butterflies that everyone loves.

—Drew Barrymore

FTER FIVE YEARS I WAS FEELING settled. I had made a few good friends. I had morphed into quite the extrovert. I was an outgoing teenager and life had turned around for me. My brother's bullying had finally stopped. Unfortunately, his hate towards me had not. We had no love between us. I always felt his aversion towards me.

I was looking forward to high school. But, once again, my parents decided to move. This time, it was to a farm outside the city. I was mad at my parents uprooting me once again. I had finally lived in a house for more than one year. When they pitched the idea of moving, I was in disbelief.

"Laura, we have decided to move to a farm outside the city," my mother told me.

"You can't be serious Mom. I am not going."

I was feisty. Rebellious.

"What about high school Mom? There is no way I am changing schools," I told her. "I'm just going into high school, and you are uprooting me?"

"You can get a school bus," Mom replied to me. "There is one that will take you right to your high school."

"I can't believe you guys are making me move again," I complained.

"Don't worry Laura, you will never miss any parties," my mother said, trying to convince me the move was going to be alright. "I promise I will drive you to wherever you need to go."

"I'd rather stay where we are Mom. The farm is forty-five minutes away from school and all my friends," I said to her.

But the decision was made. It didn't matter what I said.

We moved to the farm. I adjusted. I had learned my whole life to *adjust* to what was thrown my way. I did love the nature at the farm. It was a beautiful place.

I threw myself into prayer and meditation. I read books written about positive thinking and visualization. I started seeing my future. I was using my imagination like all the books were telling me to do. I wanted to find all the answers in life.

One day, I picked up the book *Many Mansions* written about Edgar Cayce, a psychic. He was called "The Sleeping Prophet." It was a book lying around the house that Mom was reading. I loved reading about past lives and reincarnation and how people were always living out their past deeds today. It made sense to me. I could see if someone did something in a past life, the mills of the Gods worked in perfect order. One day, you would need to experience what you had done in a previous life.

I was trying to find answers why bad things happen to good people. I had overcome such terrible childhood bullying.

I told my mother I must have done something dreadful in a previous life to deserve the terrible childhood I had. We talked about what we could have been in past lives and we guessed at different scenarios that might have happened.

I felt that I had overcome the abuse I was handed as a child.

***

I took the bus to school as Mom said. But the bus trip was never a pleasant one. I felt like I didn't belong. One time a boy sitting in the front seat turned around and opened his mouth. He had put his glass eye in it. Everyone was laughing on the bus. I just sat in my chair and got utterly grossed out. I was always so happy to get to school.

While I was sprouting in my teenage years, my brother got heavy into drugs. My friends and I were always saying what a druggie he was. He moved out of the house when I was around sixteen. It was a day of celebration for me. The days of him threatening me were finally over.

After my brother had moved out, there were a few peaceful years that I had with my parents. The land around us was awe-inspiring. I went cross-country skiing and hiking enjoying the space. Sometimes, I would sing in the fields pretending I was Julie Andrews in *Sound of Music*.

Mom seemed happy. She was involved with a small spiritual group. She wanted me to join her and be a part of *it*. I met with some people in *The Group* and listened to what they had to say. Many of them were telling me what an advanced soul I was, and that I was gifted. I could be a 'leader' they said. I knew I had some special *gifts*, but I was happy doing my own thing. And I was having some fun. I did like their meditation methods, but I didn't want to be pinned down.

Dad was enjoying the space on the farm too. He had planted many trees on our large property. Winter days, Dad was always missing because he was snow plowing the driveway from the brutal snow storms. Coming from the Gorbals, Dad enjoyed all the nature too.

So, there was some peace.

We were still living on the farm when we got a call. My brother had been arrested and caught for drug trafficking. My mom supported my brother and told him that she would always stand behind him – but he would need to change. Mom so wanted him to. My brother swore he would. Dad didn't have the same reaction. My Dad had had enough.

When my brother got married around the same time, I was excited about being a bridesmaid at his wedding. I had hoped that Mom was right saying that my brother had turned a corner. But my brother and I were living our separate lives, so if he had changed, I didn't notice. From the outside looking in, it seemed that he had.

***

I continued to become more independent. Determined to be the opposite of the shy and introverted child of my past, I continued to read many self-help books and was very diligent with my positive thinking. I kept praying and meditating. I didn't miss a day.

After graduating from high school, it was difficult for me to find a job. I figured that if I couldn't find work, I'd create my work. I decided to start a rock band. I thought I'd give it a shot.

How hard could it be to put a band together? I thought. I believed that a person determines his or her own destiny and I wanted to create my future. Not wait around for something to happen.

"I'm starting a rock band," I told my mother one day in the kitchen.

"What?"

"I think I can do it. I'm putting an ad in the paper to look for musicians," I said. "I believe I have a good voice."

I had some confidence in my singing voice. When my parents had a few friends over one night, I had grabbed my microphone. It was the kind that I hooked into the stereo, and I sang along with a record. "Bravo!" they all said and clapped their hands. "You have an amazing voice!" they said. They had asked me to sing at their son's wedding. I reluctantly agreed and sang at the church. I sang *The Rose* and *There is Love*. I had been told by many that day, that I had a talent for singing.

So, even though I had no singing lessons; I just thought I could do it.

"Do what you want Laura," Mom snapped, "but don't ever expect me to go." She walked off shaking her head.

It didn't matter to me what Mom's opinion was. I had learned to depend on no one but myself. Mom thought she would be embarrassed by my performance since she had trained professionally as a singer when she was young.

Dad helped with some financing, and I hired the musicians. Eventually, my mom relented and came over to hear my band practising in the studio.

"Geez, Laura, you do have a good voice," she said. She realized I had some singing talent after all.

My parents let my band practice at our house. It was a fun time for me. And for all of us. My parents used to come and watch the band perform. One time, Mom made the most beautiful dress for me. My dress was full of sequins and shone everywhere. I had learned a valuable lesson with all my positive thinking – I believed in myself and didn't listen to the naysayers.

I believed that I could *create* my life.

Singing gave me enormous confidence. I could stand on stage, and I had no fear. I was no longer that child hiding in my closet. And my parents seemed to be happy. But I guess children don't see everything. My parents announced they were getting divorced.

Everything changed. Again.

Chapter 18.

Eccentric

Nothing is permanent but change.

—Elbert Hubbard

MOM MOVED TO TORONTO after the divorce. It was a hard move for her. I stayed behind and lived with my father.

"This is the hardest thing I have ever done," Mom revealed. She was crying on the phone. I felt terrible.

"I'm sorry Mom, I wish I could help." I wanted to help more than I could.

"All I do is cry," Mom told me.

I felt so bad for her.

Mom called me on the phone often. We were more like sisters than mother and daughter. She would come to visit with friends she made in Toronto and watch the band performances. It was an escape for her. I knew how much Mom wanted the marriage with Dad to work. But, it never did.

I decided to follow my mother not long afterwards. The band hadn't worked out, and I wanted to move to the big city. Mom and I eventually moved into a two-bedroom apartment together. We fuddled our way through life.

The family was decimated after the split. Dad was living his life trying to find his way. Mom and I were living our lives trying to find our way. And my brother was trying to find his way too. I chose not to think about my past. As far as I was concerned, it was over. I didn't share it with anyone. I heard *time heals all wounds.* And so, I thought my wounds had been healed. I thought the past was dead.

Mom and I attended Unity Church every Sunday. It was our Sunday morning ritual. Mom was always involved in some kind of church or organization. Before she had left for Toronto, Mom left *The Group.* She decided to leave it when Dad had asked a minister to talk to a few of the members. Mom didn't like the answers the members had given the minister and decided to leave. It was a smart decision.

I enjoyed church services with my mom, but I always thought I'd find God from many different sources. Unity Church was unique to me though. They sold many different books on spirituality. And I loved the songs we sang every week; *Let There Be Peace on Earth and Let it Begin With Me* was my favourite.

Mom and I attended some palmistry courses for fun and I again heard how I should concentrate my efforts on different psychic and esoteric subjects. I was gifted. When a psychic show came to the city, I thought it would be fun to attend. I asked Mom if she wanted to go with me. We had both liked these types of subjects. We were excited to go.

We drove to the conference. It was busy. There were tables set up with many people walking around.

"Where do you want to go?" I asked Mom.

"I don't know," Mom replied. "You choose, and I'll follow."

We walked around, and I came upon a heavy-set man sitting at his table. I had a feeling he would be a good psychic. I sat down. He looked at me and smiled. We started our reading.

"You shut down and stopped communicating when you were two years old. Something happened to you," he said to me. They were the first words he said. I thought back.

"Oh yes, I was attacked by a German Shepherd," I replied. I thought it was a weird thing to mention since so many years had passed.

"You have changes coming. I see good things happening to you. You have somebody coming into your life. You've been in a dark pit, and he will lift you out. He is very tall, dark and handsome."

He was smiling and he raised his eyebrows. "This is so good for you. You've been in an awful place."

I had no idea what he was talking about. I was puzzled. I didn't think I was in an awful place. I was a bit confused by what he was saying.

He continued with his reading. "You have a very evil person around you. This person will not inflict pain on you anymore when you meet the new positive person coming into your life."

My reading was over and we left.

I was excited. I thought that was great that I would meet someone special. I really didn't know who the psychic was talking about with having an evil person around me. I never considered it could be my brother. But at the time, my past physical and psychological abuse were buried and long forgotten.

I often heard how my brother was doing through my mom. I was shocked to hear that my brother's wife had left him and taken the children. Mom told me that my brother had become addicted to cocaine and was selling the family belongings to feed the addiction.

"He has really hit rock bottom this time. He's found God and had an experience," Mom claimed.

"Wow, Mom. I hope that he has finally learned his lesson."

I believed my brother had finally changed. Being a spiritual person, I thought it could be true. I believed my mother's opinion.

After a few years passed, Mom met her new husband. He was eccentric; just like her. He was a doctor and a very different person. That worked for Mom. Mom moved into his large house in a prestigious area in Toronto. They went on many luxurious holidays – Palm Springs, Las Vegas, Hawaii, New York and Lake Tahoe to name a few. Dad had never taken Mom on many holidays. I thought it was a great change for her.

When Mom told me that she and her husband were going to take me to Palm Springs for a holiday, I was thrilled. I was living on my own, enjoying my independence. My income was limited, so taking me on a trip sounded fun. And Palm Springs was beautiful. I was grateful for the holiday.

We arrived home, and I continued to stay in close contact with Mom.

***

One morning, I woke up with one of my earplugs lodged in my right ear. I guess I had pushed it in a little too far and couldn't get it out.

I phoned Mom and told her I had a bit of a mishap.

"Let my husband get it out for you Love," Mom suggested.

"Can he do something like that?" I asked. This was not his specialty.

"Go to his office, and I'm sure he will be able to take care of it for you," Mom replied.

I headed over to Mom's husband's office.

When I arrived, Mom's husband asked me to lie down on one of his beds. He had some hesitation on how to handle my little problem. He looked inside my ear. My instinct was to walk away, but I thought I'd give him a chance to fix it.

He suggested to come over to one of his sinks. He filled up a container with cold water. He then asked me to lean over and blasted the water into my ear trying to flush it out.

The wax got wedged far in my ear; I couldn't hear. I was completely deaf in my right ear. I left feeling utterly hurt and bewildered that Mom's husband made things so much worse. I went to the hospital and waited for the Ear, Nose and Throat Physician in the emergency.

Finally, he arrived at the hospital.

I headed into the room looking around at all the specialized equipment. The doctor gently looked in my ear to see what had happened.

"It's lodged in there pretty good," he remarked shaking his head. "What the heck did you do?"

I told the physician the story.

"Well, it will take me a bit of time to get this out. Hopefully, it didn't damage your ear."

I had a sinking feeling.

The doctor took his time and much care making sure he didn't push the earplug deeper into my ear canal. He didn't want to damage it. He told me he had to be very careful to remove the lodged earplug because it had been forced further and had stuck to my ear. The doctor removed the lodged earplug piece with his instruments.

Thank God, my ear was fine. I left the hospital feeling mad at myself for letting Mom's husband do what he did. I trusted Mom's perspective and viewpoint. But she was wrong. I told my mother about the ear fiasco. Mom made light of it, and then I just tried to forget it.

***

It wasn't long after that, I met my husband. Tall. Dark. And handsome. Unlike my family, James was outspoken and said what was on his mind. He had a fierce, protective nature. I knew when I met him, he was the one the psychic was talking about.

We fell in love quickly and got engaged. We decided to have a non-denominational service in a little chapel. I wanted to keep everything simple. We invited a few friends and close family.

A year later, I was pregnant. It was a thrilling and enjoyable time for James and me. One month before my due date, we purchased a Princess Margaret Lottery Home. The family who won it had never moved in, and it was entirely new. The house was in a great city. It was perfect. Safe. Sparkling. I felt that we had found and purchased a beautiful gift. It was frantic and exciting, all at the same time.

My due date came and went. I was overdue by two weeks when my doctor decided that it was time to induce my labour.

I was in the hospital. I asked James to call my mom.

James came back to the room, he was furious. He said he heard huffs and puffs on the phone and he was shocked at Mom. Mom had asked how long the doctors thought I would be and then asked James to call her when I was close. She and her husband didn't want to stand around all day at the hospital.

It seemed to James like it was an inconvenience for Mom to come to the hospital to see her daughter having a baby.

When I had heard about Mom not coming right away, I didn't even give it a second thought. Mom's disinterest in my labour wasn't shocking to me. She was very involved with her new husband. Mom had given her power away to men for years.

When Mitchell was born, Mom came to help. She travelled every day for two weeks to help us with the new baby. We were grateful. She knitted and crocheted many little blankets for Mitchell. Mom helped out when our son was first born. After that, she didn't spend much time with him. She had told us she wasn't going to be much of a grandmother. Mom had always had said she wasn't much of a baby person. She loved teenagers much better.

But Dad was different. He loved babies. And I knew he would enjoy playing with Mitchell when he was born.

Chapter 18.

Clappa Clappa Handies

Harley was gleefully running around. Chuch, our Havanese, was barking her head off, and Teddy, our big, fat Golden Retriever was running after Harley. It was insanity – in a good way. Harley had just jumped out of our pool and was joyfully running around our yard. He ran full speed into my son and knocked him over. "Oh, my God Laura, what the hell did you do?" my husband looked at me completely bewildered.

I had always wanted to rescue a dog and Harley was the first. Harley had just been dropped off by the rescue people. He was skinny and came walking down our driveway with a little white, fuzzy toy in his mouth. "This dog is brilliant," the lady from the rescue organization had told me just a few hours earlier. "I've rescued a lot of dogs in my life, but this guy is amazing," she continued. She then told me how Harley was from the Yukon. He was tied up outside for three days at a time, without food and water, because he piddled in the house. Harley would cry and howl. A neighbour couldn't take the crying anymore. She went to the Town Council to complain. They did nothing.

The neighbour stole Harley right out of the yard and brought him to a nurse. The wonderful nurse kept Harley in her garage for five days. She then arranged to fly him down to Toronto where the rescue organization picked him up. A week later, he was posted on the internet and I fell in love with him. He was so cute with long brown fur and sand all over him from playing on the beach. He was a mutt - and a cute one. After speaking with the rescue organization, he was brought to us two hours later.

Harley won the lotto. He came into a household of people who adore dogs and he had two new dogmates. The silver spooners we called them – Chuch, our little, 10 lb. Havanese and Teddy, our Golden Retriever. Teddy had been our biggest concern.

He was a great dog, but unfortunately, along with all his bouts of diarrhea, Teddy also had "Global Fear". He was afraid of everything. When I had Teddy at one of his training classes, the trainer pulled me aside and told me to go home. Later, she told me she'd seen it before. A dog with a fear of everything. Fear that left him unable to go outside for his walks. We decided to put Teddy on Prozac.

Harley was a Godsend. He ran and played with Teddy. He taught him not to be afraid. Eventually, Teddy was taken off Prozac and lost most of his fears. And, he also lost a lot of weight.

Harley was brilliant. Fearless. He was the most precious dog you would ever meet. He would run at you at 100 mph and when he got to you, he would sit and look up. He wouldn't dream of jumping up on you. Not unless he was invited. Harley sat at my feet day and night. Everywhere I went, he followed. I don't know how many times he consoled me through sad times. Harley was there licking my tears. He understood what pain was.

When I spoke to Harley, he wagged his bum so hard his body wiggled from side to side. HIS WHOLE BODY! Harley was a lover. He loved everybody! When Harley had completed his three levels of dog training, I asked the trainer if he would be good in nursing homes. "He is an amazing dog Laura," she said, "I'll approve him for sure!" So Harley and I would go into nursing homes and he would greet all the people that couldn't get out of bed. He would run over to them in his happy way, and they would pat his head. I'd tell everyone of his courageous story.

I learned something from Harley. When you rescue an animal, you rescue yourself. It is a healing process. Giving kindness and love to Harley helped heal me.

❝ I'M HERE," DAD YELLED as he walked in the back door.

Harley came running over and Dad gave him a pat on the head.

"Hello Harley," Dad laughed petting him. "What a great dog he is."

I gave Dad a hug. It was always so nice to see him. Dad shook James' hand.

Chuch was barking and Teddy came running over. There was excitement in the air. "Grandad" was visiting.

Mitchell had been sitting on the stairs waiting for his grandad to arrive. He was four years old. Dad had always visited every week and always brought a present with him. Mitchell had been waiting with anticipation to see his grandad.

Dad gave Mitchell the fire truck he brought and then they played 'clappa clappa handies'. Dad sang and they giggled together. I took the video out and captured the special moment with them playing.

After everything settled down, Dad and I took Mitchell to the park just down the street from our house. James was preparing our supper on the barbecue.

We sat down on the bench and watched Mitchell play on the monkey bars.

Dad started to talk to me about the Gorbals and how lucky Mitchell was as he watched him.

"You have no idea what it was like when I grew up," he smiled holding my hand. "We had no green grass."

I sat listening to the story about the concrete jungle of Dad's childhood. I felt grateful for the blessed life I had with my husband and son.

Dad and I had become close after he and Mom divorced. We saw each other each week. Dad would come to visit. Dad was always trying to find the right person in his life. Dad and I had little boundaries, and unfortunately, I did have to tell Dad to stop sharing his sexual experiences with other women. I had been uncomfortable when I heard the intimate details. Dad felt bad and he respected my request. We never spoke about anything after I bridged the uncomfortable subject.

We started to walk back and Dad and I were hand-in-hand.

He started to shake his foot.

"I can't feel it," he described looking down.

"What do you mean Dad, what's going on?"

He kept shaking his foot saying it had pins and needles. I questioned him to elaborate, but he wasn't clear.

We arrived home and ate supper that James had prepared.

Dad left the next day.

Not long after that visit, I got a call. Dad had fallen and broken his leg and was in the hospital. I jumped in the car for a two-hour drive to get to my dad. When I arrived, I saw my father lying on the bed.

"How's my Dollface?" he said smiling. "I fell and broke my leg," Dad explained how he couldn't feel his foot and took a tumble onto the kitchen floor.

I shook my head. "Oh God. Really?"

"I laid there for fifteen minutes before *she* called the ambulance. She had to put on her make-up first," he responded rolling his eyes smiling at me.

We giggled.

Dad's girlfriend had a drinking problem. She and I did not see eye-to-eye. A few years earlier there was "an incident". Dad's girlfriend had a little too much to drink at Christmas. That night she slept in our larger spare room with the king size bed. Dad decided he would sleep in the smaller adjacent bedroom with the futon. He didn't want to disturb her with his snoring.

In the morning she didn't speak to me. She was very upset and cold like ice.

"Dad, what's going on?" I had asked my father.

"She seems to think you wanted me to sleep in the other room," Dad told me.

"Well, did you tell her it's not true?"

"I tried. But she won't believe me," he had said.

They left that day. My father's girlfriend and I had never spoken after that. He never fixed things.

I learned that Dad had diabetes when he was in the hospital. Dad was laying there for weeks. It was complicated because of his disease.

Unfortunately, because he was in the hospital so long, he developed a gangrenous ankle. Doctors suggested a new surgery – an "exploratory" procedure. He had two choices. One, amputate his leg.

Or two, try the new surgery. The surgical procedure would take a very good vein on the upper part of his leg and use it to replace a bad vein leading to his foot. The doctors said there was a ten percent chance it would work, and he might be able to keep his foot. Dad didn't like the idea of amputation, and my Aunt Vanna told him to try the new procedure and keep his leg. I didn't agree, but it wasn't my choice. Ultimately, it was his decision. Dad opted for the new surgery.

There were many visits and long drives. Every time I saw Dad, I heard the same thing, "Everything's alright Doll." Dad never wanted to admit anything was wrong to me. It was something my father said all the time. I don't know why he always thought that everything was okay. He always held everything in.

Dad was there for many weeks recovering.

I arrived on one of my visits to see Dad in the hospital. There was a sign on the door to put on gloves and a mask.

Dad had contracted a very contagious superbug while in the hospital. It was Vancomycin-resistant enterococci (VRE). VRE was a bacteria that had developed resistance to many antibiotics. Dad was moved to a room by himself.

I put on the gloves and mask and entered the room.

"Hi Doll," Dad said so happy to see me. "I'll be alright. It's nothing."

"Well, I don't think it's *nothing*. This is awful."

"Don't worry about the gloves and mask, Doll. It's really not that important to wear them. You can take them off."

"Dad, the nurses and doctors want us to wear them," I told him shaking my head.

Dad didn't like the protocol.

I left the hospital feeling exhausted and sad.

***

When the Easter holiday was coming up, I desperately wanted

to figure out a way that Dad could be with the family. Mom, her husband, my brother and his family were all coming. My brother had remarried and now had 2 more children.

I desperately wanted Dad to come and see everyone.

"Do you think you could pick Dad up and bring him here for Easter?" I asked James.

It would mean four hours driving for James, two hours there to pick up my father and two hours to drive him to our house for the meal. Plus, James wanted to make the turkey dinner. It would be hard, but I wondered if he would do it since I needed to be home to entertain the rest of my family.

"Not a problem," James said. "But your brother will need to drive him back to the hospital." My brother agreed to drive Dad back after dinner.

James went and picked Dad up. Dad arrived on his crutches. He was thrilled to be out of the hospital. He was a sad sight. While the family relaxed, James made a delicious turkey dinner. After supper, my parents chatted, my sister-in-law and I cleaned up, and my husband played with all the kids in the hot tub.

When it was time for Dad to go home, my brother was asleep on the couch. No one woke him up. He had fallen fast asleep at the time he was due to drive Dad back to the hospital.

"Dad has to get back to the hospital Mom," I told her. I told my mom that my brother had committed to drive Dad back.

"Your brother is so tired from all the driving he does Laura. He's always so busy."

I was hoping my mother would say something but that didn't happen.

I walked over to James.

"Your dad has to get back Laura. I'll have to drive him," James stated.

Driving at night was difficult for me. James offered to drive Dad once again. Off again for another four-hour drive. It was eight hours of driving for my husband that day along with all that cooking. But he did it for me, and more importantly, for Dad.

After Dad had recovered, his girlfriend refused to let him move back into her house. She said she couldn't handle it. I was angry at her letting Dad down when he needed her.

My protective nature kicked in and I moved Dad to a nursing home in my city. I had thought bringing him to the city where I lived would be good. I could be right there for him. Help him.

It was a difficult adjustment for Dad. The nursing home was a sad place. Even though Dad and I had regular visits, he wanted to go back home. I understood, so after six months, he moved back to his small town. It meant travelling back and forth for me, but I didn't mind and respected his decision. He moved into a retirement home.

***

I was on the phone, daily, with the doctors trying to understand what was going on. Dad was on numerous medications. Because of his diabetes, he was also having dialysis on a regular basis. Dialysis was an awful procedure – Dad was hooked up to a hemodialysis machine many times a week. Dad would tell me how uncomfortable the procedure was. I told my father I would get tested so I could give him one of my kidneys. And I suggested my brother could also get tested. He told me there was no way he would do that, and my brother wouldn't do it anyway because he was too selfish.

Dad called me. He was in the hospital.

"I'm stuck in here again," he said. He sounded frustrated.

Dad explained what happened and told me he had gone to his girlfriend's for dinner the night before.

"Did you have anything to drink?" I asked him. I suspected he had.

"Just one."

I almost dropped the phone. "Dad! You can't do that," I objected. "You are on way too many drugs!"

Dad got worse. The small hospital couldn't stabilize him. A helicopter flew Dad down to the larger hospital.

I questioned why this happened. I phoned Dad's doctors and asked them if alcohol might have been a contributing factor. They said, yes, it probably was. They said alcohol was not something Dad should ever drink – at all. I headed off to see Dad at the hospital. I rehearsed what I wanted to say to Dad's girlfriend; I suspected she would be there.

When I arrived, Dad lay staring up at the ceiling. He was completely out of it. He didn't even recognize me. I was devastated seeing him. This was not acceptable.

I needed to have a "chat" with his girlfriend. This was not going to be a pleasant conversation. I knew she was an alcoholic and her children were enablers. Not being a confrontational person, I was nervous about saying something, but this was my father.

When Dad's girlfriend arrived at the hospital, I pulled her aside with her two adult children. I had rehearsed what I wanted to say.

"No alcohol. Absolutely none. He is sick and the doctors have said it is off limits," I said calmly to her.

His girlfriend didn't appreciate the "chat". She stormed off with her two children, mad at me for saying anything to her. I didn't care. It had to be said.

Dad eventually got better and went home. He tried his very best to deal with his foot and leg. But eventually, the foot got too bad with gangrene. Dad had to come to accept that he needed his leg amputated. The exploratory procedure hadn't worked. Dad needed his leg removed just below the knee. Back down to the large hospital for Dad. And back on the road again for me.

Regular visits meant that the business I had with my husband was suffering. But I knew how much my dad needed me. James supported me and said, "Your dad needs you more Laura. I will take care of things."

I waited for Dad after surgery. I had never witnessed such pain.

Dad screamed from agony. "Phantom pain". I sat and prayed by Dad's bedside thinking, had he not gone through enough already?

When Dad got better he moved back home and into a small apartment. He had some quality of life, which had made me happy. He would ride around on his scooter and talk to all the visitors at the beach where he lived. He seemed to be much better.

***

I arranged with Dad for a visit for lunch with Chuch. It was a long drive and I was glad to get there. Chuch loved the car trips. We arrived and I gave my dad a hug. Chuch ran over to Dad.

"She's a good dog."

"I love her so much," I beamed.

"How are you holding up?"

"I'm alright Doll."

"Well, I made a little lunch for us when we go down to the water," I told him. "And I made it light. Nothing extravagant."

"I don't eat that much anyway."

Dad locked up his apartment and he drove ahead of me on his scooter. I followed in the car looking at Dad driving ahead of me. I just smiled. It was sweet to me how Dad could get around.

We arrived and I met Dad at a little park. It was a small area where there was a bench and I could sit there with Dad while we looked at the water. Chuch was free to roam. She always stayed close. No one was around but us.

We sat and looked at the lake. It was always peaceful when it was the two of us.

"How's the pain?" I asked him.

"I am managing," Dad said rubbing his leg. "It's much better since the surgery," he continued, "but the pain is always there."

"Well, at least you can get around." There was a long pause.

"I miss my leg," he said. "I loved my legs."

I felt sad for my father. Dad was always so active. He loved his golf later on in his years. He would golf often with James. Dad had always told me what a great husband I had.

We sat quietly and I pondered all that Dad had gone through the past five years. I had been there for my father through his illness. He had gone through a lot.

It had been a long and painful road for Dad with his diabetes.

"So, Mitchell couldn't come?" Dad asked.

"No, he had to work on a school assignment."

"He's a good kid."

"Yes," I replied. "We are lucky to have such a wonderful son."

"Wish I didn't have dialysis. It such an awful procedure," Dad said as he took off his prosthetic.

I didn't say anything and Dad and I ate our sandwiches.

"Do you think your Mom would ever take me back?" Dad asked. He still stayed in touch with Mom. He called her often and complained about his pain.

"Dad, she's with her new husband now," I responded. Dad had some regrets. He was lonely.

I packed up and told Dad that I better head home.

***

A few months went by. Christmas had just passed and Dad had fallen again.

The weather was bad. It was one of those years, you had to be really careful driving. The roads were icy.

Dad had hurt himself and was in pain. I had a premonition to go and see him. It was winter and it was dangerous driving, but I felt I had to get to him. He was all alone in his apartment.

When I arrived, Dad was sitting in his chair and looked very angry with me for taking so long to get there.

"Where were you? I've been sitting here waiting for you," he said looking very perturbed.

I tried to explain how bad the roads were, but that didn't seem to matter to him.

He had no food so I ran out to get some groceries. I walked up and down the aisles in a daze. He looked terrible. I just sensed the worst was about to happen.

I got back to his apartment and I helped put him to bed. He was so frail. He had lost his leg, was thin and all beat up. He hobbled to bed. I was so sad looking at him. He laid in bed and held my hand.

"I've had a good life," he said looking up to the ceiling.

"Yes, Dad you have."

"I loved that farm you know."

"I know you did Dad."

We reminisced about living on the farm. That was his favourite place. It was special to him. It was completely opposite to the Gorbals.

I tried not to cry and could feel the lump in my throat. I was so upset. I got up to get my dad some water and walked into the kitchen. I ran the water thinking how awful he looked.

"Are you going to be okay if I die?" he yelled from the bedroom.

I choked. I tried not to lose it.

"Stop it, Dad. It's up to God to make that decision." I tried to sound as strong as I could.

I took the glass of water over to my dad; we kissed and hugged goodbye. I didn't want to leave him, but I had to go back home. I drove in sadness.

The next day I woke up. The wind was blowing. It was very strong and unusual. Our power had gone out. The day was very eerie. For some odd reason, I started reading a book about a psychic who got messages from her husband who passed away after years of pain. The book, *The World to Come*, from Ruth Montgomery, was interesting to me. Ruth was a syndicated columnist in Washington before certain psychic events happened to her.

Ruth had looked after her husband for years and he thanked her in her psychic messages after he passed. I thought, *Dad would say that to me if he died. He'd see all the things I've done for him.*

I walked to the phone and called Dad to see if he was okay. There was no answer. I phoned the hospital to see if he had arrived for his dialysis.

"No Laura, he hasn't got here yet. Oh, wait, here comes the driver."

There was a long pause. Then I heard shuffling and voices.

"Sorry, Laura. Your Dad passed away last night."

I broke down. I started crying. Heart-wrenching pain. My husband and son came running over. We all hugged.

Dad had left me a note. He told me he was sorry. The pain was excruciating. He said how much he loved me and my mother. Then said, my brother too.

***

I arranged the funeral. We were blessed to have Dad's cousin come with his bagpipes. I think there is something about that sound that brings out such emotion in people.

Dad's cousin spoke. He talked about the good old times in Scotland. He spoke of the Gorbals and growing up with little around them, and of how the kids made up their own entertainment. They would come up with ways to torment each other with pranks, but it was always in good fun. He talked about how much Dad loved his homeland and wanted so desperately to go home. It was his final wishes to have his ashes flown back to Scotland.

The minister read my heartfelt letter for the funeral. I had written about our life together and how much Dad and I laughed and enjoyed life. I was grateful for him teaching me to love nature. My letter mentioned his resilient spirit and courage through all the pain he had to deal with. In the end, I thanked my Dad for who he was.

"Dad, I love you with all my heart. We'll miss you dreadfully," were my last words.

I didn't want to offend my brother and talk about how much Dad loved me, my husband and son. I didn't want my brother to be hurt. Even after all the bullying I had endured, I was protecting my abuser. I never talked about it in my letter. I was still trying to protect my brother.

The minister then read my brother's letter. It seemed very cold and lacked any emotion. My brother had had a hard time writing a goodbye letter to my father. He had kept walking around my house complaining that he had no idea what to write. I had told him to just write what was in his heart.

After the service, Mom told me that Dad's funeral was one of the best *Celebrations of Life* she had ever attended.

Along with my brother, I was a co-executor of Dad's will. It was a simple estate. Dad wanted it to be divided between my brother and myself.

My brother let me take care of the estate. There was something in the will that might have caused trouble with my brother. Dad's will stated that he wanted everything in his safety deposit box to go to me. I told my brother what it said.

"No, everything is to be divided between us," he replied to me.

I said nothing.

When I retrieved the box, it was empty. It may have contained something at some point, but it was empty when Dad died.

One of Dad's last requests was to have his sister, Aunt Vanna, take his ashes home to Scotland. My brother badly wanted to do it.

"I really want to do this," he pleaded with me.

I agreed with one condition. I told him as long as he phoned my aunt to tell her that he wanted to do it, and she agreed, I was okay with it. My brother phoned my Aunt Vanna who was none too happy with him.

She agreed, but not happily.

As each year passed, I heard the same excuse. How *busy* my brother was. Dad's ashes were waiting and waiting and I said nothing.

A seasonal business and he was *that* busy? He was given thousands of dollars to fly Dad's ashes to Scotland. He had probably spent the money. I felt terrible, but I never confronted my brother. Deep down, I was still scared of him.

"Why don't you FedEx your Dad to Scotland, Laura. Maybe you could arrange for someone to get your father over there to scatter his ashes," Mom suggested on the phone.

"Come on Mom. That is ridiculous."

"Well my husband suggested it," she chuckled.

Five years passed, and my brother *finally* decided to fly Dad home.

"Dad's finally going home," I said to Mom. "I feel terrible that it took so long for Dad to fly home."

"I know Laura, but your brother is always so busy."

"I should have said something, Mom, but I am still scared of him," I explained to her. "To let Dad's ashes wait all that time."

Inside I was seething and always wanted to tell my brother to get Dad to Scotland, but I had no courage.

My brother told me that he would text me when he was spreading my father's ashes. And he said he would send me pictures of Dad being laid to rest in Dornoch.

"That's great," I responded to my brother. "I am so glad this is finally getting done."

I never saw those pictures. And I never got that text.

Chapter 19.

You Must Forgive

The initial trauma of a young child may go underground but it will return to haunt us.

—James Garbarino

I WAS HEADING OVER to my mother's house. It was seven years since Dad had passed. Aunt Vanna had died, and I had gone no contact with my brother. The family was fractured.

"I'm coming with Chuch," I said to Mom on the car phone, "and we'll be there for lunch."

"Okay. Drive careful Darling."

"Will do."

I tried to visit Mom as often as I could. Chuch, our Havanese, was in the front seat in her doggie house. She loved her trips to Nana's house. She would look forward to meeting Mom and her four other Havanese dogs. We had bought Mom her first Havanese puppy. Mom and her husband loved the breed so much, they bought three more. It was always pandemonium when I arrived.

I travelled over to Mom's enjoying the drive. Being on the road was such a good feeling; the feeling of moving forward. It had been over twenty-five years since my parents had split up.

Years had passed, and Mom's bubble had burst. Her husband had trouble with his practice; his license had been revoked. He was found guilty of professional misconduct.

When I had skimmed over the twenty-nine-page report from the college that revoked Mom's husband's license, I asked Mom about it. Mom believed her husband was framed by other doctors who had a vendetta against him. I believed her. Even though I knew they had shredded many documents, I trusted Mom's explanation. I thought it was important to keep supporting her.

Mom stood behind her new husband, and our family did too. It was tough times, and James and I had helped Mom and her husband move. Mom had seemed happy once they settled into their new house and neighbourhood.

I arrived at Mom's house after the long drive.

I parked the car and got out. Chuch ran to the door and I could hear the dogs barking. Chuch ran ahead of me and I let her in. She was excited to see everyone.

I walked in and hugged Mom. The dogs were jumping all over me and I could hardly hear Mom as she spoke.

"How was the drive?" she asked.

"No problem. The traffic was good."

I grabbed two cookies from the cabinet. It was always the first thing I did when arriving at Mom's house. Cookies were my favourite snack as a child.

We went into the room in the back of the house. It was a glass room that Mom and her husband had built. They loved to sit there and enjoy the backyard. They had become quite reclusive over the years and loved sitting in this room.

"How are your hip and knee?" I inquired. She had been suffering from a lot of pain from arthritis.

"It's been terrible Darling. This too shall pass."

"Old."

"Ha, ha, ha," she laughed out loud.

I always knew how to make Mom laugh. I always wanted to see her happy.

Mom prepared a salad and some hamburgers while I played with the dogs. Mom's husband went outside to mow the grass and I had a chance to talk to Mom.

"Geez Mom, why don't you get a dog walker and get the dogs out once in a while," I suggested.

"Oh Laura, they love the yard. I think they are okay."

"But they need socialized Mom," I stated. "It's really good for their mental health."

Mom didn't think it was that important. Mom and her husband loved the dogs, but, I was always suggesting to her to get some training and walk them.

"I'm so proud of you," Mom said to me changing the subject. "You are such a wonderful daughter."

"Oh stop."

We sat for a while and I started to talk about my brother.

"I brought a video for you to watch. I really hope that it will help you understand all the trauma that I feel when I talk about my brother."

I had told my mother of my *awakening* after it all blew up with Vanna's estate. "No conscience, Mom," I had said her on the phone, "and he has no remorse or guilt." I was crying. I told her it made sense why I had felt so much trauma dealing with my brother about Aunt Vanna's estate. Mom had agreed with me about my conclusions. She said that she had to go through it all too.

Mom said she would watch the video with me after our lunch.

We ate and Mom's husband went to watch TV in their family room.

I was anxious to show Mom the YouTube documentary. I took out my iPad and launched the video. Mom started to watch it with me.

She looked over at me trying to empathize with me as it started. I was explaining all the things that I had learned and how damaging psychological abuse really was.

"Now I know why I married my husband Mom," I explained. "He is a truth-teller. Not a story-teller."

"Yes, that makes sense Laura," Mom nodded her head.

Mom looked at me, "Laura, you must forgive your brother if you ever want to get over your trauma."

I paused the video.

"Mom, I don't think I can do that. I have tried."

"I used the forgiveness cycle with your father." She shared the prayer that she'd said. Mom had always taught me to *forgive and forget*. Mom always taught we should forgive our enemies as the Bible said. Everything could be resolved by prayer in Mom's eyes.

I explained to my mother I would try and use the prayer, but forgiving my brother was difficult. It wasn't that easy. My trauma was real and there was only anxiety and panic when I talked about him.

I turned off the video. Mom didn't seem very interested. I felt dismayed that Mom didn't understand what I was trying to explain to her.

We finished our visit and I headed home.

I drove home discouraged that Mom didn't watch the documentary. I was fascinated by it. I finally had an understanding.

I continued to share countless books, videos and websites to help Mom understand mental disorders and psychological abuse. Mom agreed with everything I was saying to her, but I think Mom preferred to try and forget about my abusive childhood. She had a miserable marriage.

Time continued. Mom still kept in touch with my brother. It bothered me very much that she carried forward as if nothing happened.

It agitated me that my brother was always missing in action. He was always *too busy* to help when he was needed. James and I were always there for Mom. Every hardship. Every birthday. Every celebration. We were there. There was never a Mother's Day or birthday or Christmas that Mom didn't get flowers, cards or gifts. Every holiday, we had made the turkey dinner. When Mom had a hard time travelling, we brought the dinner to them.

The only time I heard of my brother visiting Mom was when he came to get supplies for his business. He would need to stay at Mom's house. She was not very involved with him, his new wife or his kids. My brother lived quite far and there were few visits.

I would hear from Mom how disappointed she always was. My brother never did anything nice for her. No birthday wishes. No asking how she was doing. He didn't care. If he cared, he didn't show it. It was always about him. I could never understand Mom staying in touch with him and I always thought he was taking advantage of her.

I would get so frustrated with Mom never telling him her true thoughts. Mom never said anything. Maybe Mom believing my brother had *found God* made her buy into the manipulations. So even though his actions were always selfish, Mom continued with her denials.

Mom told me my brother had visited with his wife and daughter and her new boyfriend. My brother spent the whole day in the kitchen cooking for everyone.

"I couldn't eat it, Laura," she complained. "The food was not any good for my stomach."

My mother had a bad stomach from surgery years earlier, but my brother, a visitor to her own home, using her kitchen, didn't even think to take that into account when he was cooking the rich meal for everyone.

"Why didn't you say something Mom?"

She never answered. It was so frustrating for me. "You never say anything!" I fumed.

Why did my mother continue to let my brother do what he wanted? What was wrong with saying to him, "My stomach is bad dear, I can't eat that type of food." Was it because my brother knew very much how to manipulate my mother? Because she had promised to stand behind him all those years ago and because it was something she could never forget? Could it be my brother knew how to use that promise against her? My Dad was never there as a child, did my brother use that?

I hoped my mother would eventually *get it*. But Mom was always complicit. There were always secrets with my brother. And this one really upset me.

It had been a lifetime of lies, manipulations and schemes. And a lifetime of secrets and ignoring problems. Secrets and problems that were all disclosed when administering my Aunt Vanna's estate.

Chapter 20.

Entangled

Controllers, abusers, and manipulative people don't question themselves. They don't ask themselves if the problem is them. They always say the problem is someone else.

—Darlene Ouimet

A T LONG LAST, I got the news. After nine long months of trying to identify my aunt with multiple DNA tests, Aunt Vanna was finally identified. The medical examiner's office in New York was beyond busy. The employees were extremely difficult to deal with. It was a lot of phone calls and work. Vanna's death certificate was finally sent to me.

I got all my forms ready to send to the Surrogate Court. My plan all along was to send the death certificate to New York and apply to have them administer Vanna's estate. I planned to mail the package the next day and went to bed.

I woke up in the morning out of a really strong dream of Vanna. Being a spiritual person my whole life, I have had many answers come to me from my dreams.

"Hun, wake up," I whispered to my husband.

"What's up?"

"I have to tell you about my dream. It was so strong and vivid."

I told James what the dream was.

I was at work and was given a painting from my Aunt Vanna. Then I received some kind of code. I figured out that I needed to turn the painting around. There was parchment paper that I needed to remove. After I removed it there were three envelopes attached to the painting. I started to tear off the three envelopes on the back of the painting. All were secretly hidden. They opened up to all the savings. There was a picture of my aunt looking at me. She was about seventeen in the picture. Young. Looking up. She said that she put everything into her savings. I told her how sorry I was that we didn't keep in touch. Then I woke up.

It might have been my aunt telling me that she wanted me to look after her estate. I wasn't sure. I started to get signs and messages to do it.

I felt hesitant to do it because I didn't want to deal with my brother. Deep down, I still had not dealt with the anxiety I felt. The buried fear I had of him. I didn't want to push my blood pressure up, but something was still telling me to take care of the estate.

I decided to phone a lawyer in New York who was affiliated with the funeral home where we had arranged for Vanna to be buried. The funeral home had looked after the burial pro bono. If the estate was settled later and there was money from the estate, they would get paid for their services at that time. The lawyer and I worked out our agreement.

Now, I needed my brother to just stay away from me. I did not want to get triggered again.

As a last resort, I decided to ask my mother to help. I knew Mom never liked getting entangled in our family disputes. Her words, "Don't get *me* involved," had been drilled in my head. Right or wrong never seemed to matter to her. She never wanted to take sides because my brother would use emotional blackmail saying Mom was taking my side and how much more Mom loved me.

But even though Mom was always *neutral*, I asked her if she would call my brother to let him know that I was applying to administer the estate. I just wanted him to keep his distance. I was hoping that with her agreeing on my brother's mental health issues, things might have changed.

Didn't happen.

Unfortunately, the call did not go as planned.

Mom called me.

"Your brother doesn't want you to administer the estate," my mom said deflated.

"God Mom. Why not? For crying out loud Mom, what happened?" I was again feeling extreme frustration.

"He said that James *controls* you," Mom remarked.

Projection! The very thing my brother used to do to me. *Control me.* Mother, defeated as always, bought into his mind games and deceptions once again. She did not help, as usual.

I reacted right away.

"Oh Lord, Mom. James has a big and loud personality," I indicated. "But he **absolutely** does not *control* me!"

Over the years, James and I had had our share of arguments like any married couple. But, he never *controlled* me. I had to learn that arguing is something normal and always had a difficult time with the arguments. I had a really hard time controlling my emotions and would feel down for days. But we worked through our disagreements.

With my parents never allowing me to *raise my voice*, I had always thought arguing wasn't a good thing. I had to learn that people need to talk, talk *very* loudly, even *argue* about their issues and work things out. Burying issues doesn't work.

True to form, my brother, once again, had *projected* his own controlling personality onto someone else – my husband. Knowing James was extremely outspoken, and knowing Mom had always liked to keep things quiet and didn't like any "voices raised", my brother twisted that on Mom. My husband was his great scapegoat.

"Geez Mom, you are easy prey," I grunted.

My brother had manipulated my mother saying, once again, Mom was *on my side*. He pulled out all the manipulative tactics he could think of. He went into full throttle. Blame, false accusations, emotional blackmail, projection and scapegoating. My brother always knew what buttons to push with Mom.

Just like before, when I was trying to administer my Aunt Vanna's estate, my brother was sneaky, calculating and conniving. He charmed Mom and she didn't see it. My brother had always said things so sweetly. So softly. His whole life he sounded so sweet while *lying* to my mother.

After I pointed out the truth to Mom, she agreed and could see that she had been conned. Mom felt bad and wrote my husband, "Hey just off the phone with Laura and I certainly do NOT think that you control her! You have a VERY strong personality but she is very strong too."

Mom said that she had always seen James and I discuss our issues, then agree to a resolution. She assured James that she knew he did *not* control me as my brother had inferred.

After my mother spoke to my brother, my brother decided to phone my lawyer. He had the lawyer's details from Mom.

After the call, my lawyer phoned me.

"Geez, Laura, your brother sounds like a really nice guy on the phone."

"Yes, the wolf in sheep's clothing. He does *sound* nice."

I wasn't surprised. That's what I had experienced my whole life. Other people seeing the mask. The sweet face.

"Your brother asked why you would get four percent for administering the estate," my lawyer continued, "and I told him that it was the normal amount for someone looking after an estate. He didn't like it."

"Nothing surprises me."

"Your brother would like you to drop the four percent."

"Wow, that's crazy," I replied.

"I really don't recommend it, Laura. This will be a lot of work."

My brother had mentioned nothing about my husband *controlling* me as he did to my mother. *Only* the money. His jealousy and greediness became very clear to me. I think my successful life had been horribly difficult for him.

My lawyer continued telling me about his phone conversation with my brother. He had suggested to my brother that he could come to court or have another lawyer contest my application, in court, if he wanted.

My lawyer told me he asked my brother if he ever had a criminal record. "No," was his immediate answer. He lied, not disclosing his drug trafficking and felony convictions. My brother told him that he had checked police records, and there was nothing showing up on their systems.

When I got off the phone I told my husband what the lawyer said.

"Why on earth would anyone check police records if they've never had a criminal record in the first place?" James pointed out.

Only then did I realize, that's right!

I didn't even realize the manipulation of my lawyer.

I immediately called my lawyer back. We talked again. I told him what my husband had mentioned to me.

"No one needs to check police records if they've never had trouble with the law. I've never had a parking ticket in my life. I certainly don't have to check any records," I told him.

He gasped. "You're right Laura. That never even occurred to me." From then on my lawyer knew what he was dealing with.

***

When my husband heard about all the manipulation that was going on, James felt compelled to write to my mother. He understood she never wanted to get involved, but he wrote her. He suggested that it was time to say something. At some point, you have to do what's right.

James asked Mom if she was going to allow her son, my brother, to discredit me in court and try and stop me from doing the *right* thing.

For over twenty years, I'd had a successful marketing business and worked with government clients. I drank very little alcohol. For years, I had volunteered to help abused animals. And I had looked after my sick father and my father's estate. Being a trustworthy person, my brother couldn't discredit me but he certainly could try. He would have to prove I was a drug addict, prostitute or had some sort of criminal background.

My husband's email motivated Mom to write to my brother. It was the only time my mother actually did the right thing by saying something to her son. She said the truth. I couldn't believe it.

Mom sent a message to my brother and then shared it with me.

Her tone was angry. She said that she was **not on my side** like he had said, and what he was doing was wrong. She said it was decided by everyone, in the beginning, that I was going to administer the estate.

Mom also listed the many things he did wrong throughout this process: your sister never received the cheque; the DNA took forever; DNA would have taken ten minutes; excuses – you were so busy; two seconds to pick up the phone to tell your sister the cheque would take time; everyone was waiting; your sister asked you to stop emailing, but you kept coming at her with no respect for her wishes; you shared private information which was written to your cousin in confidence – not right; you are giving your sister a hard time about four percent, which the lawyer has recommended not to do; by all accounts, Aunt Vanna wanted your sister to be sole beneficiary; to lie to the lawyer about your conviction was wrong – the right response was to say, yes, it was over forty years ago; your sister is trying to get over her horrible years as a child and you are doing your best to bring it back to her memory, and; she was sorry my brother's wife had to deal with this as she is sick with cancer and he should be focusing on and helping her.

In her final line in the email, Mom told my brother to do what was right, or she would remove him from her will.

I was amazed. Mom had never said anything to him like that before. I'm sure when he received that email, he must have been completely mystified. I was completely relieved when I read the email. Mom really came through.

I called right away.

"I cannot believe you wrote that Mom."

"Well, let's hope he does it and will let you do what you need to do," she replied.

I was so glad Mom finally said something. It was about right and wrong. She stood up for what was right. I hoped she finally would stop being manipulated by her son.

Not long after that, I received an unexpected email. It was a letter Mom had written to my brother's wife. She hadn't sent it and wanted my opinion. She wanted my brother's wife to know about my childhood abuse and to know my husband did not control me.

The email said she had to *step in and stop all the nonsense.* Mom confirmed my brother abused me in my childhood and that he had threatened and terrorized me. She said that she hadn't noticed the abuse.

"She used to sleep in a little closet and not come out and was so introverted all through her life. It wasn't till I gave her piano lesson with a very dear friend, a school teacher that she came out and talked and got the help she needed in later years," she continued.

My husband did not control me, she said, but he did have a *very strong* personality and wanted to protect me.

"My son can think what he likes about Laura but the truth is she is a very caring and giving person and it is too bad he cannot remember what a dreadful childhood he gave her threatening her and terrorizing her so that she could not confide in her parents and retreated to her own little world to survive."

Mom's email ended with stating that she loved her son and supported him no matter what he went through, but she felt she had to *take sides* in this situation. She really didn't want to.

Both Mom and I felt bad for my brother's wife because, along with cancer, she was dealing with isolation. My brother had moved them to a house trailer far away from their family and friends. Because things were difficult enough for her, I suggested that Mom not send the email.

My mother was finally willing to tell the secrets, but I stopped her. A bad decision!

But I still have that email – evidence from my own mother of my abusive childhood. I keep it in a nice safe place.

***

Vanna was finally buried. The service was conducted by a rabbi from the funeral home. My lawyer went to the Surrogate Court to see if there was an approval for my application for administering my Aunt Vanna's estate. There were no issues.

I was assigned the administration papers for Aunt Vanna's estate.

I was co-fiduciary with the lawyer in New York who was simply amazing. We worked hard together for a year and a half.

It was not an easy estate to administer. There were a lot of phone calls to find my aunt's hidden bank accounts. Because it took so long to identify my Aunt Vanna, all the contents of the apartment went to the dumpsters. My aunt's apartment was completely demolished and destroyed. Her whole life and all her life's history was thrown away into the trash. It was so unfortunate.

Over the months, there were *numerous* documents, visits to lawyers, notarizing letters, phone calls and investigation.

And as time passed and while I worked hard on the estate, I didn't realize my brother was slowly maneuvering his way back into my mother's life. Mom never told my brother to leave her alone. That wasn't her way. Sweep everything under the rug, ignore it, and it will go away was our family philosophy.

I had thought my mother would keep her distance until the estate was closed. But she didn't. I warned her there would be issues, but she ignored me.

So, my brother, the master manipulator, after being threatened, was turning it up a notch, worse than ever when he was allowed back into my mother's life. He made sure he was sweeter than he'd ever been. He needed to make sure Mother would never reprimand him again.

With Mom and her husband having some wealth, it wouldn't be very good if Mom took my brother out of the will – like she had threatened.

Chapter 21.

The Ultimate Hurt

To those who abuse: the sin is yours, the crime is yours and the shame is yours. To those who protect the perpetrators: blaming the victim only masks the evil within, making you as guilty as those who abuse. Stand up for the innocent or go down with the rest.

—Flora Jessop

AS THE MONTHS PASSED, nothing changed. Mom didn't say anything to my brother. I guess deep down, I sensed she would not stay true and hold to her words. She had never protected me when I was an innocent little girl. But I hoped that things would change because I had finally concluded that my brother had a mental health illness. Mom had agreed.

A year and a half had passed and Aunt Adena, Dad's youngest sister, had decided to come for a visit to Canada. Adena was a very special person. She was the opposite of her sister Vanna. Kind and caring, Adena spent her retirement years volunteering in hospitals.

We were close when I was little before we moved to Canada. Aunt Adena and I had always kept in touch. Every year, we sent cards to each other. I sent her videos of my family. After Aunt Vanna died, Aunt Adena and I had written often and we became even closer.

Aunt Adena arrived. James and I picked her up from the airport. She was very proud of herself flying to Canada, as she had a fear of flying for years. She was so excited. I gave my aunt a big hug. It had been years since I had seen her. We talked about her flight and we drove Aunt Adena to Mom's house. She was going to stay at Moms for a visit.

James and I dropped Aunt Adena to visit Mom.

My aunt was visiting my mother when I got the call from the lawyer saying that the release documents for the estate were ready to be signed. How wonderful that she was in Canada when it happened. All the waiting and all the work were finally over.

It was also good timing for me to take over hosting my aunt, as my mother was having a difficult time with the visit. Mom and her husband had become quite antisocial over the last few years and Mom was having a hard time with her very energetic visitor. Mom was also having a hard time dealing with the death of one of her dogs from months earlier.

I was getting ready to pick up Adena when the email came in. My brother had spoken to my mother. Mom's email said that my brother was "happy" but he didn't know when he would sign the release, as he was *extremely busy*.

I reacted immediately. A surge went through my whole body.

Mom's email set me off and completely triggered me. I had worked on this estate for a year and a half with the lawyer, and the estate was ready to close. All my brother had to do was simply sign the papers with his lawyer and we would get our cheques and close the estate. *Extremely busy* could mean how long with this liar? He was unpredictable.

I wrote Mom back, "Well hopefully he doesn't wait to get it done like he did last time. I really hope you said something... He will cause issues again."

I told Mom I had worked hard on the estate. It had not been easy. There was no response.

I picked up the phone and phoned my mother. I was not going to let it go.

I was upset – something I was never allowed to be. I was so irate that my brother was *too busy* once again. He had used this before when he didn't send the cheque. And he used the same excuse for waiting five years with my father's ashes. I was beside myself.

"I hope you said something Mom. He is using the same excuse again!"

"I don't want to hear about it," Mom snapped at me with a cold and angry tone.

I had an immediate reaction of dread. It was just like when I was a child. Her words completely brought back my past; how I was ignored. This was the straw that broke the camel's back.

Mom completely shut me down. Again, she was buying his excuses.

I couldn't believe it. She didn't want to hear about it? My brother, with his manipulations, had done it again! All these years later. Mom, couldn't see what she was doing.

As I travelled over to my mother's place to get my aunt, I was *really* annoyed. My anger had bubbled to the surface. I wrote to my mother and said she needed to call my brother and get him to sign the papers. After all my years of dealing with this perilous abuser and his manipulation of my mother, my anger had seethed to the top. For the first time in my life, I was angry. *Really* angry. I had been taught to stuff everything down and not talk about it. Bury everything. Not this time! *I'd had enough!*

I arrived at my mother's. I walked in.

"Did you get my email?" Mom looked very angry with me. I had broken one of the rules. Never get angry with my mother.

"Yes."

I had expected my mom to finally see what had been going on. But she was in huge denial. Mom never wanted to *get involved*. I think she really resented me for getting her involved in the whole situation.

Oh, for heaven's sake, there is right and wrong in this world. *You take the side of right!*

"What the hell Mom?" I yelled. "Do you not remember what happened before?"

I grabbed my aunt's suitcase after raising my voice at my mother and walked out.

On my way home, I heard from my aunt how Mom had talked about my brother so admiringly. He was a fantastic cook. He was great at his job. Really?!?

Flabbergasted. I was astounded my mother had not been truthful. She had told me she would have a heart-to-heart with my aunt. My brother may be good at his job and a great cook, but what about what we had discussed? Not that he has a mental illness that will continue his whole life or that he manipulates everyone for his own selfish ends? Not that he tortured animals and threatened my life as a little girl? Not that I had trauma talking about my brother because of his threats? Not that he is a troubled person causing havoc in our lives? Not that he's applying for welfare? Not any of that?

Mom's protection and enabling of him continued.

I felt so betrayed.

***

A few days later, I received an ecard from my mother for my anniversary. It was a day late, but that was okay. The message said *Happy Anniversary* and that was it. There was no mention of what happened.

Old patterns of ignoring everything and it will go away slapped me in the face. No way! I needed to talk about it. Fifty-five freakin' years of abuse had boiled to the top.

I wrote to my mother. I let her know that I had calmed down and how hurt I felt.

"...I don't think you realize how listening to my brother telling you how 'extremely busy' he is set it off terribly. And then you give me that in an email thinking I would not get upset ????"

I told Mom she had forgotten all the issues that happened a few years ago. "When I read your email, I called and tried to talk to you about it and you would not hear me out at all. That was very upsetting!" I wrote begging for validation.

I told Mom she was getting sucked back into my brother's manipulations again.

I asked her, "Why did you not talk to my aunt about his sickness? You told me you would have a heart-to-heart. But instead, you tell her he is a fabulous cook? What are you doing mom?"

I told Mom that she was being a hypocrite, that she was saying one thing and doing another. My email continued on about how hurt, sad and disappointed I was. I said that every time my brother was around, there were always problems.

I then included part of the message she had sent to my brother a year and a half ago. The only time my mother did the right thing.

There was no response.

Silence.

***

After the visit, my aunt headed back to England. Aunt Adena gave me a big hug and thanked me for suggesting that she stay involved with Vanna's estate. She was so grateful I had recommended that she take a share of the money for her children.

The estate was signed off. It was finally done and settled.

I had heard nothing from my mother.

I phoned. We spoke. Mom still didn't get it. She said she could not surmount this fight. I told her that there was nothing to surmount. Just see it for what it was, admit she was sucked in again and let's get on with life. She said she was too old for this. She just couldn't take it.

She then said the most bizarre things. It was goodbye to me. She said I had the money and things seemed good in my life.

"What has that got to do with any of this?" I objected.

This was nothing to do with the money! This was the same complicity between my brother and mother that had been going on my whole lifetime. The same emotional neglect – my mother making light of my brother's actions and completely ignoring the trouble he caused. No consequences. All coming back into my life again.

My mother's complete inability to deal with issues resurfaced. Mom thinking my brother would change if she supported him, was deep in her psyche. All the years of my brother using emotional blackmail had worked.

Mom's final words were, "Let's pray on it."

Mom was sticking her head in the sand.

I sent three more emails desperately imploring my mother to be aware of what she was doing. I wanted some kind of acknowledgement. I asked for an apology.

I tried to explain how hurt I was. Just like when we were kids, I was trying to get my mother to hear me. She refused to listen to me. Refused to empathize with me. Here I was, a grown-up woman, and the same thing was happening.

No reply.

Silence.

***

After the silence, I finally wrote an email saying that I wanted to hear from Mom or I would need to make some decisions. I refused to take the silent treatment Mom was giving me.

Mom wrote.

The first line in that awful email stated that she had finally found *enough stomach* to read my emails. I felt queasy reading it.

After I read the first line, I knew nothing had changed. There was no awareness of what she'd done. There was only a defence that my brother did everything that was asked of him. My mother was, once again, defending my abuser.

"Oh, God!" I whispered.

Half-way down the email was a dismal apology that she was sorry I was hurt by what she said – she wanted to talk "positively" to my aunt about my brother. Mom then stated that she only spoke to my brother once a month and thought that threatening to take him out of her will would prove her love for me. She also said she was willing to go to a lawyer and notarize a letter that my brother had psychologically abused me as a child.

The end of the message Mom stated that she wanted to have a stress-free life. She wanted me to know that if this wasn't acceptable, I would need to take some steps and decisions. She ended with how much she loved me.

Mom said she loved me, but where was the action to back it up? I had always wanted her to *protect* me from my brother who bullied me. *That's what mothers are supposed to do.*

My brother threatened my life! I had trauma from it! I wanted her to see that there was right and wrong; bully and victim.

I responded once again saying how hurt I was. All I *ever* wanted was protection from this abuser. I never got her protection when I was abused as a child and I wanted it now. I desperately needed a mother. Not a sister.

Silence.

***

As time passed, my son's 19th birthday was fast approaching. It was a very important birthday for him. Surely my mother would send him a card as she had always done. I went to the mailbox every day, and every day I left heartbroken.

My son's birthday arrived. There it was. A birthday message on Facebook. I could only shake my head. Disappointed, once more.

I was heart-broken. So much sadness. And now, I had to come to terms with reality. That my mother was not there for me. Mom had only been there as long as I played her game of pretend. As long as I didn't ask her to take on a role of "mother", then everything was okay. No matter what she said, my brother had never changed. I was no longer willing to participate in the charade. The pretense we had a great family. And her not talking to me and stonewalling me, broke my heart.

This was a deal-breaker for me.

So, I gave Mom peace, as she wanted.

Chapter 22.

Validation

After darkness comes the light.

—NEPOS

T HE WHOLE SITUATION completely devastated me. My mother had turned her back on me. After all these years, Mom slammed the door in my face. I couldn't accept it. I had trusted her.

I went and visited my family physician. I talked to my doctor about the mental disorder I thought my brother might have. My doctor's reaction was amazing to me. "No conscience," she explained. She shook her head. "It's the worst kind of illness."

I felt relief. *Finally, someone who understood.* It was like a light bulb went on.

"It's not like schizophrenia," she continued, "these people don't know they are sick." I talked to my doctor in great length about how it affected the family. She was so understanding.

After our talk, I decided it was time I got help. It was time I dealt with my post-traumatic stress disorder symptoms. I was experiencing these symptoms every time I talked about my brother to anyone that wanted to listen. When I would try to tell friends what happened dealing with my aunt's estate and with my brother, I found myself full of anxiety. I felt pressure in my chest. I felt panic. My arms were shaking. I had a huge intense fear.

I desperately needed help.

***

It was important to find a psychologist in my time of need, but more importantly, one who understood psychological disorders when dealing with both psychological and physical abuse. I was determined to find a therapist who specialized in this type of abuse. A therapist who understood trauma from childhood. I was lucky enough to find one.

When I first met Farrah, I really liked her. She had a true warmth about her. Farrah told me that we were going to go on a journey together and I would experience many emotions. Her first concern was my health. Peeling back the layers were going to take a lot of courage.

"I'm really scared Farrah," I trembled, "I've buried the abuse and I'm afraid of what I'll find." She understood.

"It's a journey and we will take it slowly. I just want to make sure you are taking care of yourself. I want you to always be safe," she assured me.

And so, we started on the quest to my healing. I started to talk about the abuse.

Farrah was a Godsend. She furthered my understanding of

personality disorders and I started to see how the whole family is affected by people with toxic behaviour. I knew Farrah could not make a concrete diagnosis without seeing someone, but she validated my thoughts on how terribly concerning my brother's behaviour was.

Farrah validated all the feelings that I was denied for years. I learned how harmful psychological abuse actually was. My family had thought it was nothing.

My extreme symptoms of trauma from my brother's threats made sense. As a child, it was toxic stress for a long period of time. So, I finally got some true understanding. I wasn't crazy. I was a victim of remorseless, psychological and physical abuse. Threats to my life were very damaging. It was abuse that was sneaky. No cuts, no bruises.

It was a shock to me when Farrah told me I had Post-Traumatic Stress Disorder. Farrah went into great detail about Complex Post-Traumatic Stress Disorder; what it was and how it compared to PTSD. I had never heard of it.

"Complex PTSD is not a diagnostic DSM disorder. It is defined by its cumulative effect."

I listened and I started to feel another *AHA* moment coming.

"Often with PTSD there is the traumatic event; perhaps someone was in the war or had a car accident. With Complex PTSD, it's more when we see psychological abuse. It's this accumulation over time of feeling threatened."

"Oh my God, that is incredible."

"Someone may ask, well what was the traumatic event? But it was a variety of abuses that happened over time that significantly shape the person. They end up with the same symptoms. They end up with hyper-arousal to trauma cues. They feel physically stressed. Their blood pressure increases and all that kind of stuff."

"Right." I felt a sense of relief.

"So people avoid trauma cues," she continued. "And, so when I work with people who have had psychological abuse, that's what I see. That complex picture."

"Yes, Farrah, this is all so great," I said smiling.

I started to understand why I had such terrible PTSD symptoms when dealing with my brother.

"Why are most of my memories gone?" I asked.

"When the situation is threatening and when the situation creates arousal, you are not a relaxed kid. You are not a calm person," she explained. "Your baseline is elevated. You are living in a threat state. Your body perceives the threat."

"That makes sense to me."

"So what that means, is your sympathetic nervous system is turned on."

"Yes," I nodded.

"That is the system that turns on when we need to fight or flight. It is the emotional centre of the brain. So what is fascinating about the threat system, is that everything changes. It's not just your brain. It's not just your memories. Your eyesight changes. You actually don't see as well," she went on.

I was sitting trying to take in all the information. I was finally *getting it.*

"You can't scream or yell as loud because your vocal cords are restricted. Your hearing is modified. You can hear things close to you but not long distance. So when you ask me, Laura, why don't you remember things and why your memories are disjointed, it's because when you're in threat system and arousal is high, you cannot remember things in a logical way."

"Wow, Farrah, simply enlightening."

"It's very difficult for experiences to move from short-term memory to long-term memory. They get stored in really disjointed ways; if they get stored at all," Farrah said in her sensitive way. "The body is in survival mode."

I sat and just shook my head. So much information that helped.

And Farrah talked about boundaries and how toxic families are missing healthy ones. In toxic families, children are an extension of their parents. There is no separation.

"So, Laura, if you make your family look good, then they are very proud of you. And, if you act in a way that they don't approve of, they will cut you right off."

"Just like my mother did."

Farrah looked at me and nodded. "And that's not what healthy families do."

***

Week by week I learned. I journaled. I healed.

But a strange thing happened in my sessions with Farrah. I found out about family and all its dynamics.

"How can my mother keep protecting him?" I asked Farrah. My heart was aching.

"Most times families will protect the abuser," Farrah told me. "I see this quite a lot."

"But she was close to me. I was betrayed. I trusted her!"

"You have a right to feel mad," she acknowledged.

"So I'm on my own then? How can my mother just stop talking to me?" I cried. My tears were streaming down my face.

Farrah looked at me with compassion in her eyes.

"I don't know."

I shared pictures to Farrah of when I was a child.

"How come that little girl wasn't protected from her bully?" I asked her. I felt so much pain. "Look at that little girl! My poor Little Laura was not protected!" I sobbed through my salty tears. "And my mother thinks that prayer is going to resolve this? That makes me so mad. She wants me to forgive my brother or I'll never get over my trauma."

Farrah understood. She explained to me about how trauma

is trapped in your brain. She went into great detail about how our emotions are changed by trauma; how our brain is changed by trauma.

"How am I going to release this trauma?" I asked.

"With evidence-based therapy. We will gently release the trauma by exposing it. We are going to talk about this Laura," Farrah said in her assuring way. "Gently and safely."

I felt so good.

There was such comfort in being heard. And being heard by someone who understood psychological abuse.

"My husband has always protected me. He has been my protector, thank God. I was always brought up not to raise my voice and how terrible it was."

I told Farrah about my husband's very assertive nature; his loud personality.

"Laura, there is a big difference when you compare having disagreements and a loud personality, to someone who is intentionally wanting to hurt you."

"I know Farrah and my husband has been the great scapegoat because he calls out the truth."

"The difference Laura, is we all make mistakes, but having remorse and empathy afterwards is key."

Coming from such an abusive childhood, I started to understand my hypersensitivity to arguments and the fear I felt. Every time I argued, it hurt so terribly. I was on high alert. I was hypervigilant. Hypersensitive. There was a connection in my brain from the past threats as a child.

I learned how trauma in our childhood can affect the part of our brain that makes us fear more. The Amygdala becomes enlarged. I had become wired for fear.

It was so great learning that there is an enormous difference when you compare an argument and disagreement, to outright lies, threats on safety, deceitfulness, manipulation and control.

I could now see the difference when I looked at my childhood. There was direct *intention* to harm me. Hurt me. Lies were said to hurt me *intentionally*.

"People that lie, manipulate and play with other people's minds, can drive someone to snap Laura," she said with her compassionate voice. "I am trying to educate the court systems to help them understand the importance of psychological abuse. Help them understand which abusive behaviours would be signs of a personality disorder."

"Really?"

"The courts are making decisions about the lives of children. And often there is equal custody and access given to the children. The effects are long-term on children who are subjected to psychological abuse by a parent. And quite often the abusive party can show up in court as so sweet and accommodating."

"Oh that is just so awful."

"Quite often the healthy parent gets passed as the unstable one because they are upset. They are terrified. A lot of them have PTSD," Farrah explained.

It was horrifying for me to hear what can happen in these family disputes.

Farrah understood how my husband snapped at my brother and could completely understand his anger.

"It's normal for people to get angry with the incessant lying and denying of truth. Have you heard of gaslighting?" she asked.

"Never heard of it."

Farrah went into detail about gaslighting and what it was. She told me about the movie *Gaslight* and suggested to watch it.

"The movie is about a husband who makes great efforts to coerce his wife into thinking she is going crazy." Farrah explained more on what manipulation is. Twisting of truth. Playing mind games.

In my many sessions, I learned that the physical abuse that my family had considered so inconsequential, was actually abusive.

Tickle torture was just that. Torture. It was non-consensual physical abuse. Holding me down, restraining me and controlling me was physical abuse. Licking someone's face with vile breath was abusive.

"I completely shudder when I think of the hedge shears," I told her. "They make me so nervous."

"Cruelty to animals is not *normal*. And witnessing that abuse was psychologically harmful," Farrah explained.

I started to see why I felt panic. Fear. My life was threatened! I had no protection from an abusive person who thought he could control and do anything to me. It caused me to shut down and hide in my closet. Nightmares beyond my young mind's understanding. It was all so damaging to my psyche. I was in survival mode.

I started to face my demons.

I learned how secrets go hand-in-hand with family abuse. There is a lot of shame and guilt involved.

I learned about how families keep secrets. There was now some understanding of why my brother's wife had never answered me when I had asked her about my brother blaming her for the cheque not arriving for my Aunt Vanna's estate. I also learned that isolating someone like my sister-in-law is a control technique that Farrah sees quite frequently with people who perpetrate psychological abuse.

I also started to come to terms with my mother who decided to turn away from me. It was devastating. I was in such mental anguish over my mother.

"I feel like I've been punched in the stomach," I described. Farrah told me that the silent treatment has the same chemical reaction in a brain, as someone being punched.

"Some psychologists say it is the worst type of emotional abuse."

"That explains my pain."

"Have you heard of the term 'flying monkeys'?" Farrah asked.

"No, I haven't."

I remembered the Wicked Witch of the West and her flying monkeys in the *Wizard of Oz*. I learned in psychology circles, flying monkeys is a common term. The flying monkeys work on behalf of the abusers, doing all their dirty work, enabling them. When the flying monkeys return, they are rewarded by the abuser. I concluded my mother was a flying monkey. And I suppose, up until the blow-up with my aunt's estate, so was I.

Farrah and I discussed covert emotional incest. Being too close to a parent is not healthy parenting. It is not healthy when a parent confides in their child to meet their own emotional needs. I told Farrah that I had to tell my father to stop talking to me about his sexual experiences after he and Mom divorced. I had no idea.

I then asked Farrah, "Why didn't my brother sexually abuse me?" The thought made me feel very uncomfortable even asking it.

"Not all people with predatory behaviour are sexual abusers."

"Maybe if he had, my mother would have done something."

"But would she have believed you?" Farrah asked me tilting her head.

"I don't know. And that is a good question."

I kept asking questions.

"So why do people keep associating with abusers?" I asked Farrah.

"Sometimes it takes one good act, or a person saying, 'I'll be good, I've changed.' Then we forgive. Good-hearted people forgive," she said.

I could relate to this. I believed the lies and was easily deceived.

Farrah went into detail about patterns. Psychologists will make a diagnosis from patterns; patterns of behaviour.

It was all so enlightening.

"I thought I had all the answers," I commented. "Now I realize, I don't. I never knew I had buried so much, and I want to learn everything. Ask the right questions."

"That is great Laura."

I was so grateful I was getting help.

I finally started to see the big picture.

Chapter 23.

Meeting Little Laura

Dissociated trauma memories don't reveal themselves like ordinary memories. Like pieces of a puzzle, they escape the primitive part of our brain where the trauma has been stored without words.

These starkly vivid and detailed images are defined by our five senses and emotions, but there is no "story". So we are left trying to comprehend the incomprehensible while trying to describe what doesn't make sense.

—Jeanne McElvaney, *Spirit Unbroken: Abby's Story*

F ARRAH AND I CONTINUED TO WORK on my healing. I talked to Farrah about a therapy that I thought might help. I wanted to write with crayons with my non-dominant hand. Dr. Lucia Capacchione wrote a book called *Recovery of Your Inner Child*, a self-help book about writing with your non-dominant hand using crayons. I thought that it would be a good way for me to hear my little, hidden and terrified inner child. Farrah thought it was a great idea.

And so, Little Laura and I communicated. For the first time in my life, I finally started to hear my inner voice, Little Laura, who was neglected, ignored, abused. Little Laura wrote to me with her crayons and told me her unbelievable story. What a wise little girl she is.

I heard a voice that made me cry. Every day.

Little Laura asked,

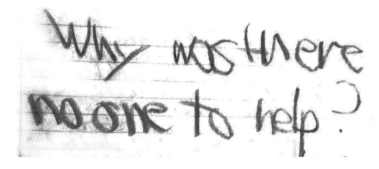

My heart broke.

Little Laura told me how terrible she felt. How scared she was of my brother,

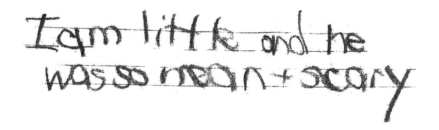

Connecting with my little, hidden child had profound results. Conversations we had are a story in themselves. They were illuminating. My little girl never lied to me, and I heard how she saw my grown-up life. I became pretty proud of myself, seeing my life through my little girl's eyes. She was so happy to see my success.

I asked Little Laura how she felt that Mom wasn't talking to us,

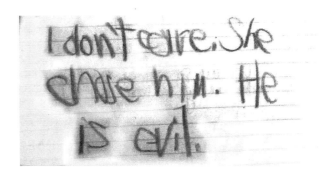

I don't care. She chose him. He is evil.

Little Laura was the child hiding in her closet. She was so terrified. Abused. Neglected. Alone.

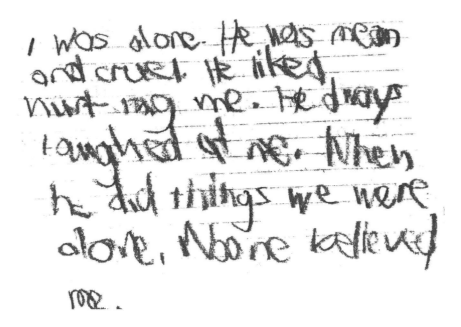

I was alone. He was mean and cruel. He liked hurting me. He always laughed at me. When he did things we were alone. No one believed me.

I became aware of Little Laura's story. She had never been heard. Her pain didn't matter. She was always ignored and never had a voice. Her pain was always trivialized.

Little Laura said that she was very angry with my mother. We are born so innocent. Unfortunately, some parents make mistakes. They are not perfect. We live in a very imperfect world.

I was older now and I knew it is up to me to become the parent to my injured child and heal myself from the abuse. It was important that my inner child spoke out. It was important I finally heard what she had wanted to say for decades. I became the parent she never had. I became the protector she needed.

I started to expose the trauma and I became very brave. My little girl inside got very scared when I decided to confront my brother with a letter.

I assured her I would never do anything to hurt her and make her sad.

She told me,

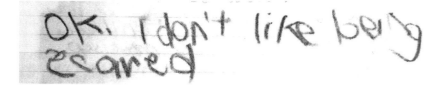

Chapter 24.

Facing My Biggest Fear

💬 *"You seemed really strong to me in high-school," Sherry said. Sherry was a girl I knew in high-school that I hadn't seen for ten years. We met up in my twenties when she moved to the same city that I lived in. "Really? I did? I don't see myself that way," I replied. We continued to talk and reminisce about our years in high-school. I started to think back to a job I had when I was just seventeen.*

I had taken a part-time job at a small motel and worked evenings – the night shift. I would work the front desk checking people in for the night. The foyer was extremely small and there were no other people around and, back in the '70s, there were no security cameras. I was never scared about being on my own and I never thought anything "bad" would ever happen.

It was about midnight. It was a quiet night. Two young girls walked in. They had jet-black hair and had sunglasses on. They couldn't have been much older than I was. I knew something was wrong right away.

The first girl walked up to me. She had a knife and held it to up to my neck. She told me they just wanted the money and to cooperate. I had no fear. I opened the cash register and said, "Here you go." It was not a lot of money – mostly one-dollar bills.

They grabbed the money that was in the register and ran out. I calmly called the police who showed up minutes later. I gave them my account of what happened and was completely calm through it all.

The whole incident didn't seem to have any effect on me. I went home to bed and the next day phoned the motel to talk to the woman working at the front desk. She told me that one of the men that had checked out of the motel that morning, a conductor on the CN passenger train, had seen two girls buying tickets with one-dollar bills. He had called the motel to tell them what he witnessed. "Did anyone call the police?" I asked her. "I don't think so," she replied, "the train has already left."

I called the police and I told them the story – that the two girls that robbed the motel might be on the train. The police stopped the train at the next stop. They arrested the girls. I was pretty happy that I had been so brave and that I had reported what I knew to police.

Months later, I had to go to court to identify the two girls. They were sitting in a crowd of people and I walked in front of the crowd and was asked to identify them. Their hair was no longer black, and there were no sunglasses. But, I took my time and identified them.

Maybe Sherry was right. I was strong after all.

A S I STARTED TO GET SOME understanding and courage to look at my past, I realized I wanted to face my brother, my abuser. I chose to call him out for all his cruelty. I chose to let him know what I thought he was and release him. He was fooling me no more! His final manipulation of my mother drove me to do it.

I told Farrah I wanted to send a letter to my brother.

"He held me down forcing his cruelty on me and I want to be lifted out. It is time I stood up to him. He thought nothing of my life. I want to show how much I love myself and my inner child. I want to show that he can no longer control me and fool me," I told her.

I wasn't going to keep the secrets buried anymore.

"Laura, there are not too many people that can do what you want to do. It takes a lot of courage to face an abuser," Farrah informed me. "When you do send a letter, it changes the dynamics of relationships and others need to change too."

Farrah supported me and wanted me to do it if I felt safe enough.

Farrah had seen a lot of relationships change within a family once someone takes a stand and speaks out. She said that she had no idea what would happen after I sent my letter.

I thought it was important. My brother had caused so much pain in my life and I *refused* to be silent any more. No more secrets!

My first letter was nothing but anger. It was emotional. I read it to my husband. Tears were streaming down my face.

"It's good Laura. It's all emotion," James said. "You're not really saying anything that happened. Why don't you state the facts? Try again."

I rewrote it – a twelve-page letter to my brother stating all the physical and psychological abuse. It took a week and I was determined to send it. The letter was factual. I wrote about the tortured animals, the frogs, the snakes, the birds, the licking my face, the physical abuse, the threats on my life, the manipulation and lies with my aunt's estate, the five years with my father's ashes. It told my brother I had an awakening and what my true thoughts were. I told him my conclusion; that he had a mental illness.

At the same time that I was writing the letter, I continued writing with my non-dominant hand. Little Laura was scared. She was terrified of sending the letter. My post-traumatic stress symptoms were high. My brother had threatened to *kill* Little Laura if she ever told and this was a tell-all letter. I was also sending copies to my brother's adult children.

Little Laura and I continued to write about the abuse and how she felt as a child. She wrote that she thought her brother would come and "get" her.

I started to see how the little me, my authentic self, really felt. It was so sad. She felt no one was there for her. No one protected her. Sending the letter was something I knew that I had to do. I had to do it for her! She deserved that. My whole life I had kept secrets.

Farrah thought it was a good idea to send the letter, so I had support.

***

Even though I felt compelled to send my letter, I found it was not that easy. I was experiencing trauma. I thought my brother would come to find me and kill me. I was *telling*. I was doing exactly what he threatened he'd kill me for doing.

I continued to breathe. Every time the panic attacks came, I kept breathing. All my years of meditation helped. Every time I panicked, I used mindfulness. It got me through.

I did something I had not done for years: I picked up my Bible. I needed help. I kept reading Psalms. Certain passages gave me strength. Psalms 27:1 was completely uplifting: "The Lord is my light and my salvation; Whom shall I fear? The Lord is the strength of my life; Of whom shall I be afraid?"

Psalms was a story about overcoming evil, and I believed that was what I was doing. Overcoming evil. I continued to read Psalms 31:24,

"Be of good courage, And He shall strengthen your heart, All you who hope in the Lord." I was finding courage.

To me, there was no word other than *evil* that describes a person who gets pleasure from bullying. Someone who has *no conscience*. All those years, I had someone playing with and manipulating my mind. This person cared about nothing except himself. He had no regard for life.

As I continued to read how much I was loved by my Divine Creator, I found courage. I felt no one could take my life away. I was born from spirit, and now, I needed to have faith. Faith in myself. I needed to do this for Little Laura. I had never stood up to this bully.

I may have had to live in fear when I was little, and now I wanted to end the fear. End the abuse! I had support from my loving husband and son. They kept telling me how much they loved me and would protect me. Even though I knew they were there, Little Laura still panicked. She needed to be consoled and loved. I continued to do that. I told my inner child, Little Laura, that she was being so brave.

I remembered *The Color Purple*; how I watched it and got inspired. Sophia found the letters her sister wrote her for years. Letters her abuser hid from her. She found out that her long-lost sister is living with her two children and Sophia finds the courage to leave her abuser.

The scene at the kitchen table was completely empowering and uplifting. Sophia's abuser is told she is leaving, he tries to bring her down. He tells Sophia she's ugly, and all she's good for is being a maid. He keeps berating her. She snaps! "*Until you do right by me, everything you think about is going to crumble,*" Sophia says holding the knife to his neck. She walks away. He yells to her that she's black! She's poor! She's ugly! She's a woman! She's nothing at all! She walks out and repeats her words. Sophia has stood up to her abuser after years of abuse. I was inspired!

I'm strong. I am powerful. I am going to do this through my fear, I said to myself. I was alone at my computer. I took a deep breath.

I shook. I trembled. I took slow breaths. I needed to do it. Even though I was fearful, I kept praying. I kept breathing. Then... I pushed the send button.

It was *gone*!!!

I couldn't believe I did it. So many years of hidden abuse were exposed with one little "send" button. The most empowering part of my letter was the last page, reclaiming my power:

66 HEALING

So, what is this letter about? This letter is about truth and having the courage to tell my story. It's not about revenge. That's not who I am.

Today I choose to reclaim the power you took from me. I release all the shame and guilt for not defending myself against you. I release all my sadness over not being protected and not being able to protect myself. I release the hatred that I had of you.

NO longer do you have any power over me. I am free of your manipulations. I take back my power and relinquish yours. I decide who I have in my life and embrace my beautiful true little self that deserves all the love in the world.

I decide to walk in this world as a fully giving, loving, peaceful human being, loving my family, continuing to rescue animals (who I've learned can heal from abuse like I have had to), and do continuous acts of kindness to other human beings. God sees my truth. So do I.

I choose to not have you in my life. Whatever contract and karma I had to come to this earth to work out, is done with you.

Germany, after all their genocide, teach the children about the evil that their elders did on innocent people. Without talking, there is no healing. Your children are now grown up. Have spouses. Have children. This email is cc-ing them, the emails I do have. (Your wife is not included due to her health issues.) They need to know the truth.

You have told everyone my husband has control over me, and has caused the upset between you and I. I think people will feel differently after reading this.

And on a last note, I have documents filed with my lawyer, 2 doctors, my psychologist, the police. I have letters from friends and family. Documents are power. Don't contact me. Don't even try.

Your sister"

The letter to my brother was gone. I finally *told*. I had released my secrets and stood up to the bully and all his wasted space.

It was a long time coming.

***

At the same time, I sent my mother an emotional letter letting her know that I had been seeing a psychologist. I told her no more lies and no more secrets. It was time, to tell the truth and do what was right. I told her how much I loved her and waited for her call. I told her that I wrote a letter to my brother. She had received a blind copy.

❝ I am no longer keeping secrets inside that are causing me very strong negative reactions. I had to get in touch with my little child within, Little Laura, and listen to her. She has been stuffed away for years. She deserves some attention and protection. I have had to listen to her terrible ordeal and cry with her. My Little Laura is not pleased with you. You never listened to her."

I mentioned the Facebook message to my son and how it exacerbated our situation. Then I tried to explain my pain:

❝ You have refused to understand my pain. You had a mother that protected you. I did not have the luxury of a protector. And was hoping things changed. They have not. You are continuing the lie, like I did with my abuser. And by continuing the lie, you continue the abuse. It was bad enough you didn't protect me when I was a child, and I forgave you for that. But now it's different.

I told my mother that even though she had agreed with me on my conclusions of my brother's mental health issues, she continued the secrets and pretended like everything was the same.

I wrote Mom that she never had the heart-to-heart talk with my aunt like she had told me she would.

"Are you willing to keep playing along and lose the daughter you should protect?" I asked.

I told Mom that I hoped that she would have the courage to talk to my brother when he calls and tell him the truth.

    " My phone number and email are still waiting. I know you want peace in your life. Peace cannot follow until one faces the truth, stops keeping the family secrets. This is not about revenge for me. I hope you know that. It's about truth, and having the courage to tell it."

In the end, I told my mom how much I loved her, missed her and I hoped she understood what I had to do.

I desperately wanted Mom to step up. This letter was my last hope.

I gave my mother a chance to finally stand up for what's right. It was her time to come to terms with the fact that she had a child with mental health issues and do what she should have done a long time ago. I had hoped so much she would. It is not often people get second chances in their life to right the wrongs they have done.

She wrote. She said she received the letters and to stay well.

That was it. Nothing else. At first, when I received her four-word email, I thought it was communication opening up. I asked her to explain herself.

Stonewalled.

Everything went silent.

***

Now I had to deal with my mother's betrayal. Nothing from my mother! All the courage to finally stand up to my abuser and she cut me off. She refused to help. She refused to stand behind me. Mom's mom had protected her so much as a child, Mom had decided to do the opposite. Offer **no** protection.

I had no idea what would happen after sending my letter. No one wrote. It was silence.

I had panic attacks. I sat looking outside my window and waves of anxiety came over me. I guess, deep in my subconscious, there was still the fear that my brother would kill me if I ever told anyone about what he was doing. I'd been told that my whole childhood. Now I had told.

I felt huge waves of fear. Panic filled my body. I kept looking out the front window to make sure no one was there. I had to stop myself thinking my brother was going to hunt me down and find me. I had to continually stop past fears and terror from coming into my mind.

As the panic feelings continued, I turned to the methods I knew. Methods that had got me through tough times over my years. Practicing the present moment and a lot of prayers. I kept praying and reading my Bible. It was really helping. I had faith that what I was finally doing was the right thing. Little Laura and I wrote every day. I listened to her story. I consoled her.

Not only was it difficult dealing with my panic attacks, but I also kept crying about how my mother abandoned me in such a difficult time of need. Then I'd remember how my brother had manipulated her, her whole life.

I went for a visit to see Farrah. I shared my letters.

"I did it," I exclaimed. I was nervous.

"Laura, what happened?" Farrah asked me.

I told Farrah what I did. She was so amazed. Farrah helped me with my panic attacks and gave me some suggestions to help with my fears.

We talked about my mother's response and I showed Farrah the four-word email. She shook her head.

"What goes through a parent's mind when dealing w horrific child? I am sure it's difficult, but at some point, y come to terms with it and protect the others from the pe predatory behaviour," I said to her.

"Honestly, Farrah, I didn't think I'd ever see the day that I would set boundaries and stand my ground. I always had a huge fear of doing that. The message was loud and clear, *Let's not talk about it and everything will be okay*. Well, everything was not okay. I refuse to accept abuse and I refuse to live by someone else's rules. I needed to protect the innocent child within me that never had protection before. Now I have spoken out," I said proudly.

Farrah asked me what sending the letter did for me. I told her that, first, I felt I had finally stood up to my brother and ended the secrets. And second, I wanted to see if my mother would finally do what a mother should. Protect me.

I found out my answers.

I had to now accept the horrifying truth; my mother was never there for me.

It was only an illusion.

Chapter 25.

Finding God?

I was playing with Mitchell on the floor with his toys and games and I went to get up. Something popped in my knee. I couldn't move. The pain was excruciating. I made it over to the couch and said to James that I needed an ambulance. James called our neighbour who came over to look after Mitchell.

The ambulance came and I was admitted to emergency. I had no idea what I had done. I couldn't walk and needed to be lifted everywhere. They wheeled me off to get an x-ray and put me onto the steel table. "What happened?" the technician asked. "I have no idea," I replied and told her how this just came out of nowhere. She left me alone and told me to stay very still while she went into a separate room to take the x-ray.

I closed my eyes and asked for help. I stayed still and visualized the Universe surrounding me – helping me. I imagined Jesus helping me. Boom! My leg took an enormous jump. It lifted right off of the table. The technician came running over to me. "What was that?" she asked in shock, "In all my years, I have never seen anything like that." She went and took the x-ray.

I got up and walked out. James met me outside the room. "What's going on? How come you're walking?", he asked. I told my husband my weird story.

There was no explaining it. It was one of the mysterious wonderful things that have been going on in my life. Doctors told me it must have been a ligament that snapped back into place on the table.

A FTER THE BETRAYAL AND SILENCE, I did a lot of soul-searching. I did a lot of thinking about "God". Having prayed and having so much faith my whole life, I realized there was more to figuring out life than I had thought.

"I am so proud of you and your brother," Mom once told me. "You have both found God and that is the most important thing to me. If there is anything I can be proud of in my life, it's that both my children have found God."

My brother had found a sweet spot. And used it. With my mother, finding God was important to her. Mom had always thought prayer was going to resolve all the problems; fix things. I pondered the scene from the chilling movie *Carrie*. Carrie comes home full of pig's blood from her prom. The bullies at her school had collected pig's blood and placed it above the auditorium stage. They rigged the election and Carrie gets crowned the Prom Queen. They pull the rope and the blood comes tumbling down on Carrie. After using her telekinesis to kill everyone in the auditorium whom she thought was behind her assault, she goes home. Her mother hugs Carrie and rocks her saying they will pray together. No. I didn't come home covered in blood like the movie. But the scenario was the same.

Prayer was not going to fix a lifetime of lies and secrets. There is a time for prayer – and this wasn't it.

It's a very tender and sensitive subject – *God. Spotlight* won an Academy Award highlighting how *God* had been used for all the wrong reasons. Many spiritual leaders of our time prefer not to say the word *God* because there have been so many horrible and hideous acts committed in the name of *God.*

Cruelty, death, war ... all in the name of *God.*

I decided to have a discussion with a PhD with extensive experience in the federal prison system, I wanted to learn as much as I could about mental illness. We had a lengthy discussion about psychological disorders and also a discussion about God.

"I can't tell you how many times I've heard from these guys, that they have found God," he said. "I was always wondering what God was doing hanging around the prisons," he joked. We laughed.

I had wondered why my brother was lying, denying, sabotaging and manipulating if he had found God.

I questioned to myself how people might like my brother. Could they not see through his shallow ways? Could they not see through his soft, sweet voice? A charmer. A con. I guess not.

When it all began with Aunt Vanna's estate, my brother had called my Aunt Adena. "How's my *favourite* aunt," he said. My aunt had told me, afterward, she felt uncomfortable hearing this. My brother had not been in touch with her for over forty-five years. I could only shake my head when I heard what he said. It was so insincere. It was easy for me to see the *other* side.

But, I realized that most people are so trusting. Honest people believe that others are telling them the truth. Unsuspecting, they believe other people are being honest like they are. A charmer knows what to say to people to make them feel good. A charmer has a calm voice. He sounds sincere. A wolf in sheep's clothing.

Underneath the facade is someone that is only concerned with himself. Everything has an ulterior motive. But, at some point, a person has to look past the mask. Look past the charm. *Saying* that you are spiritual, *saying* you have found God, *saying* that you are a great person, does **not** make you a great person!!

Just because someone says something, doesn't make it true!

I think after all my questioning what "God" is, I concluded it all comes down to empathy.

Empathy for others. Being kind and loving to ourselves. And that needs to happen when we are children.

Chapter 26.

Reflecting Back: We Both Needed Help

You can't go back and change the beginning, but you can start where you are and change the ending.

—C.S. Lewis

FTER MY REFLECTION ON "GOD", I started to reflect on my childhood years.
Looking back, I realized that both my brother and I needed professional help.

Hiding in my closet to keep safe from being terrorized and unprotected, I needed a psychologist – not to be thrown outside to fend for myself, and asked to keep silent about schemes to catch my brother in his never-ending lies. I really needed a doctor after my parents had turned a blind eye to how the physical and psychological abuse was affecting me.

I so wanted my mother to confront my brother in front of me and call him out for the abuse and lies – not be sneaky. I so wanted protection – not further secrets. I think my mother eventually gave up trying to catch my brother with his lies. He only seemed to get worse after getting involved with drugs and started skipping school.

Unfortunately, I had endured years of physical and psychological abuse before getting any help. My mother told me years later that she would come into my bedroom while I was sleeping and ask me to forgive her. She had failed to help me all those years. I did forgive her all those years ago.

And, my brother? Unfortunately, his insidious, sadistic behaviour never got treated. I concluded that the years of ignoring and making light of his lies, cruelty and lack of empathy only enabled him, empowered him and made him a better liar.

I had many questions going through my mind.

What kind of pain was my brother in that he needed to inflict so much pain and suffering on me?

When my brother and I had plantar warts on our feet, Mom took both of us to the doctor to have them removed. I remember my brother screaming and screaming out loud when they inserted the six-inch needle into his foot. When it was my turn, I didn't make a noise. Tears ran down my face as I remained silent. It's interesting how my brother dealt with his pain on the outside and I dealt with mine internally.

Why did my parents not get treatment for him? Did they not want to admit there was a problem? How could they not see his behaviour was extreme? How could they not take him to a doctor? Did they think my brother would just grow out of it?

I wondered if I was supposed to feel sorry for my brother, my abuser because my parents didn't get psychological help for him. Perhaps.

It's true my brother never formed strong bonds with my parents because he was with my grandparents for most of the time until he was three. But, that didn't mean he should have been allowed to get away with such terrible, abusive behaviour. Many children have different caregivers when they are infants, but do not become abusive.

I concluded that my parents' inability to *manage* my brother and *ignoring* his deviant behaviour escalated my brother's feelings of self-importance and entitlement over the years.

A child that lies continually, who lacks empathy, who has no remorse for misbehaving, who is self-entitled and sneaky, who abuses animals needs professional help! There was a cry for help under all my brother's bullying behaviour and it was ignored or excused. It wasn't handled at the critical time in his young life when it *might* have made a difference.

Unfortunately, I read that there are many studies that show children displaying this type of behaviour have a high risk of graduating into abusive adults and perhaps, developing a devastating personality disorder.

But I had other questions.

Why didn't my parents protect me, an innocent little girl, from getting bullied by a brother with such cruel behaviour?

And does my mother's choice to enable my brother in my adult years, resolve any of my family of origin's problems?

It was troubling. All this pretending. My mother always said to me, she didn't do enough in our childhoods; but nothing good can come out of enabling and protecting an abusive person.

What about my father? Is it because my grandmother allowed him to bully his youngest sister he thought it was alright for my brother to bully me?

I had never talked to Dad about my childhood. He was never a great communicator. And I never talked to my father why he wanted to be with his friends instead of his children and family. My dad knew my brother had terrible challenges, yet he never protected me. I never asked Dad the important questions.

I have forgiven my father for not protecting and being there for me as a child. At the very least, he recognized my brother was deeply flawed. After my brother was convicted of drug trafficking, Dad started to really see through the manipulation and lies. Unlike my mother, he had distanced himself from his son after my brother got in trouble with the law. It was too much for him. He never got past that one. Perhaps, Dad finally realized that it wasn't "just sibling rivalry" after all. My brother didn't grow out of it as Dad had hoped.

On reflection, it seems my trauma, neglect and bullying had gone on for many, many years. Through many generations. Ultimately, I was lead to the most important question:

How do I turn this pain and suffering into something positive?

This pain must have a purpose.

Chapter 27.

Finding Purpose

I contacted a psychic after it all blew up with my brother. "Do you have a lot of eagles that fly around your house?" the psychic asked. "Yes, I live in a place with a lot of eagles," I replied. "You have eagles all around you," she went on. "You have animals all around you." I answered her, "I'm not surprised; I've had dogs my whole life."

"No Laura," she said, "I'm talking about many other animals. Not just those ones. There are many more," she continued. I was very intrigued. What did she mean?

"You have wolves, eagles and other animals, all surrounding you," she said. "If anyone was ever to try and hurt you, these spirit animals are there protecting you," she said. "This is all from your past life as a Native. You healed many animals in that life," she continued.

I was definitely interested in what she was saying. I have loved horses, dogs and animals my whole life. I cannot seem to get enough of nature. I watch animals and birds and I have been rescuing dogs and cats in my adult years. I knew I had always loved animals, so this all felt right.

She continued, "You have two important spirit guides. There is a chief and another Native woman, a medicine woman – a healer. This Native woman was teaching you in your past life how to use your hands to heal. These two spiritual guides are always with you." I thought back to when I was a child. I had many clothes that looked Native American. And then I thought about how much I loved Native art and music. Interesting.

The psychic then told me to think about starting to use my hands. I had healing hands. I could heal people if I wanted. I knew I was a person who enjoyed praying, but this was something new. When writing this book, a thought crossed my mind. I looked at my hands. Could my psychic have meant that this book could help heal people? My hands, writing my story?

Maybe.

" I WON'T BE TOO LONG," I yelled to my husband. I had arranged to meet Sandra. Sandra's family and my family were close when I lived on Prestwood Road and the farm. Both of our families had moved to the farm and we had lost touch after I graduated high school.

When I learned that Sandra lived only twenty minutes away, I called her. We had talked numerous times on the phone but we finally met up for coffee. I hadn't seen her for years and we were excited to see each other.

We hugged. Sandra hadn't changed at all. I could see her brilliant, blue eyes as soon as she walked in.

We went and got our coffee and cake. We sat down; we were so happy to see each other. Giddy.

Sandra and I shared what had been happening in our lives. There was so much to catch up on. We exchanged a few photos of our children and dogs. I sat and thought how so much time had passed. We were grown up women with our kids in university.

I talked to Sandra about all my rescue dogs and cats; how much it meant to me to help animals later on in my life.

We eventually started to talk about our childhoods.

"God, Sandra, how did we get through our early years?"

"I don't know, Laura. It was terrible."

We laughed.

I told Sandra about what finally happened with Aunt Vanna's estate. She knew a little bit after Vanna passed away. It led to Sandra telling me about Lydia's passing. Sandra was executor for her estate.

I told Sandra what Lydia did when I was nine.

"Thank God Lydia helped me out, Sandra. She was the one that saved me as far as I'm concerned."

"I didn't know any of this," she looked at me surprised hearing my story.

"There are some people that show up in your life who are extraordinary and make a difference. Lydia was one of those people." I had a little tear in my eye.

"What would have happened to me if Lydia didn't help me when she did? It's frightening for me to think about it. I feel terrible that I missed the chance to thank her for recognizing that I needed help."

Sandra and I reminisced about Lynne, her sister. Lynne had also passed away from brain cancer. Sandra told me how their mom wasn't going to visit Lynne, even as she was dying.

"Lynne waited until they finally came. She hung on until they arrived at the hospital."

I had tears in my eyes listening to the sad story.

"Did you know that Lydia was going to adopt Lynne when my mother didn't want her?" she asked.

"No, I didn't know that." I felt terrible about it. "Poor Lynne. I guess I wasn't the only one Lydia tried to help."

I told Sandra about the time Lynne and I were playing and she broke my collarbone. Lynne had come to the hospital with my mother and heard me scream when they lifted my arm to cast it. Lynne had felt so much guilt. Sandra had no idea it happened.

I changed the subject.

"So, I've been dealing with my Mom no longer speaking to me."

"Oh Laura, you guys were so close."

"Yes. Too close."

I told Sandra the long story of what happened.

"I wanted my mom to tell the truth about my childhood and my brother. She preferred to shut me out of her life. I've been stonewalled. She has made the choice to keep enabling my brother. All these years later and she keeps continuing to protect him!"

"Shocking."

"Thanks."

We continued talking about our childhood memories.

"I had no broken bones. No bruises. No cuts. But my psychological cuts went deep. All these years later, I have started to understand the trauma I felt when I talked about my brother."

Sandra just sat and listened while I explained my trauma symptoms and that I had been diagnosed with PTSD.

"I had thought I was going crazy. No one ever believed me. As a child, I always had a feeling of insanity inside. Just because I had no physical signs of abuse, I was made to feel the abuse was nothing."

"Do you remember the pink bellies I use to get from your brother? He held me down and slapped my stomach until it turned to beat red."

"That's bad. I got the tickle torture and the licking my face after Marmite."

Sandra made a face, "Oh God! That's horrible!"

"I know. Thinking about it, just grosses me out. And my parents did nothing."

We talked about the *frogs* and how awful we both felt thinking about it.

"I went home nauseated after I saw your brother blow up the frogs," she described.

"Horrible."

"And what about the dead pigeon?" Sandra asked.

We laughed at the insanity of it all.

"I've grown Sandra," I told her sipping my coffee, "and now I'm working out the fear." I went into great detail about the causes of trauma.

"Amazing."

We sat quietly for a minute.

"So, how do you feel about your Mom not talking to you?" Sandra asked knowing I felt so sad about it.

I took a deep breath and looked out the window.

"It's been really hard. But, there is nothing I feel I can do," I replied. "It's about setting my boundaries and listening to my inner child."

Sandra agreed how important it was to heal.

"Takes us a long time to figure things out and realize we must live for our own true selves. I've started to put my little self first."

We both got up and filled our coffee cups. We walked back to our table enjoying each other's company.

"All I really wanted, was some validation for my pain," I said to Sandra, "and I think my mom just doesn't understand the trauma that I had. She still thinks that sticks and stones are the only things that can hurt you. Words are no big deal."

Sandra shook her head.

Sandra and I talked about *The Group* and how her parents were still involved in it. They had abandoned her at seventeen and she had to fend for herself because they had moved to Toronto to be with *The Group*. Sandra had no food and ate at her boyfriend's house just to have a decent meal.

"Pathetic, and just wrong. God is great Sandra, but it looks like God keeps getting used in a way that makes no sense to me. My mom's last words to me were to pray on it."

Sandra just shook her head.

"I just recently a read a quote from St. Francis of Assisi." I pulled out my iPhone. "*It is no use walking anywhere to preach unless our walking is our preaching,*" I read.

"That's a good one," Sandra smiled.

"So I guess a lot of people can say they are spiritual, but show me for heaven's sake."

"I agree with you."

"Just last night I watched a YouTube video. A woman talked about her near-death experience. She had been fixated on her looks and had abused her body with diet pills. When she had her experience, she was given a very important message. All the little things she had done over the years – all the random acts of kindness – mattered. Not winning the gold medal at the cheerleading competitions. Not the things that she thought were so important. It was the things she did each day for others. Helping a little old lady across the street. It is the acts of goodwill, the selfless acts, which show a person's true goodness and character. **Godliness** is when we exhibit kindness and love for others," I said with passion.

"You are so right, Laura," she answered sipping her coffee.

"And, man, if my brother found God, his actions sure said otherwise."

Sandra understood. She agreed with everything I was saying.

"Have you heard how your Mom is doing?" Sandra asked.

"I heard she took a trip to Hawaii," I answered. "I'm really not sure if she will find the peace she's looking for."

We continued to talk and I told Sandra all about the healing process with my little girl. My small, innocent child, Little Laura. I told her how we've cried together and hugged together. We have laughed together. After all those years that she dare not speak, I had finally had given her a voice.

"I feel I've embraced the Little Me," I explained, "and I'm finally loving myself. That's what the Universe wants me to do."

Sandra and I talked for hours. It was so nice to hear that somebody remembered how crazy my childhood was.

Sandra and I hugged goodbye and said we would never lose touch again.

Chapter 28.

Peace

And the day came when the risk to remain tight in a bud was more painful than the risk it took to blossom.

—Anais Nin

I GOT HOME AND DECIDED TO TAKE Loo for a walk. I wanted to reflect further on all that had recently gone on in my life.

Loo and I crossed the street and walked to our favourite spot in the field. I watched Loo run and enjoy her freedom.

We played for a bit and Loo came and sat with me.

I took out my iPhone. I decided to narrate a message to my five-year-old self. Little Laura. I recited my message on my iPhone as I sat in the field,

    " Hi, Little Laura.

As I sit here contemplating the last few years, I can't believe how my life has changed.

I never listened to you for decades. I'm sorry about that.

I've heard it said that calling out family members for their abuse is the highest level of principle. The letter to your brother was not about vengeance. It was about truth and having the courage to face my bully. He hurt you. No one cared. He intimidated you and threatened your life. You were a little girl with nowhere to go."

Tears were streaming down my face. Loo just sat looking at me panting.

    " Mom thought being sister-like was acceptable. We needed her to be a mother. She didn't want to or she didn't know how. I'm still not sure which one it was.

I know how much you desperately wanted your brother's love. That never happened. I don't think he will ever love us. Mom and Dad needed to ensure that bond formed when you came home as a baby.

So, I have had to accept that it won't ever happen, as sad as that makes me. I guess maybe one day I will hear from your brother's children. The secrets and abuse will continue on for them, I suppose.

I heard that your brother believes I am making horrible claims about him and causing stress for the family.

Yes, I've made my own suppositions about your brother. He will never go to a psychologist for a diagnosis. Why would he? He doesn't think he has a problem. I will say, with Vanna's passing I saw the similarities between the brother you knew and the brother I know, and I have arrived at my own conclusion.

I guess at the end of the day, it doesn't matter.

It's more important that we heal the PTSD from all the abuse and neglect.

I've decided I'm going to tell your story. All the journaling I've done, and all the times we've talked, I think it's time to speak up.

I think people should know what kind of terrible, concerning behaviours are extremely hurtful. Maybe by reading your story, people will not accept abuse themselves. Not accept lies. Maybe they will set their own boundaries and become whole as we did. It would be your story, my Little Laura. A story about truth.

You did nothing wrong, my dear child. I am here for you now. Thank you for being so courageous.

We have turned into a survivor. We have stopped the cycle of generations of abuse."

I hugged myself. Anyone looking would have thought I was crazy.

I got up and started walking home with Loo.

"That's it, Loo. I'm going to do it. I'm going to write it all in a book. I want to talk about my truth. I want to heal wounds. I hold no resentments. Do I have all the answers? No. I'm a work in progress girl, aren't I?" I said to her as we walked together.

"You know Loo, us humans, I think we all could write a book about our lives. Our lives are books. But I think I'm going to write about mine."

It was just Loo and I walking in the forest. Only my voice and our footsteps could be heard.

"Who writes about abusive siblings?" She just kept walking enjoying our little walk.

"Who writes about the silent abuse and child emotional neglect?" I asked her.

We kept walking.

I remembered a great quote, as we continued:

> *You own everything that happened to you. Tell your stories. If people wanted you to write warmly about them, they should have behaved better.* —Anne Lamott

We arrived home. It was time I had the courage to tell.

I grabbed a pen and paper. I wrote down the goal of my book:

Psychological abuse and child neglect. They are crippling and need to stop.

Chapter 29.

The Walk

We park the car and get out. It is dusk and it's in the middle of winter. It's one of those nights that I want to package up in a box. The sky is completely clear and there is a sliver of the moon left. Beside the tiny moon are some stars that are waiting for their recognition. Both my husband and I have decided to go for a walk with Lou, our wonderful rescue dog. She patiently waits in anticipation of where we will take her. This is one of her special walks. It was going to be long, not one her shorter walks just across the street. That walk is nice, but this is going to be a nice, long one down at the waterfront.

When we arrive, a few people are feeding the ducks. There are thousands of them quacking loudly. There's a woman holding her little pail of birdseed that she bought for the ducks. They surround her and she is squatting down, feeding them. They must be hungry. There is one large swan feeding right out of her hand. The woman isn't dressed in anything too fancy. Her coat is old and a bit ragged. I comment to James, "They're not putting this on CNN. She obviously doesn't have a lot of money but she has spent some of it to feed the ducks." My husband pulls Lou close not to upset the scene we're watching.

There is a ski hill in the distance with all the lights starting to come on, and there is a large bay of water at the bottom of the mountain. The waterfront has been renovated with paths and large street lights running all along it.

We start our walk along the waterfront. The sun is just disappearing behind the mountain. We look over and there is a beautiful, yellow sky as the sun says goodbye for the night. Panning over to the water, it is glistening in the night. The clouds are turning blue, purple and pink. It's completely peaceful.

There are very few walkers along the trail. The snow is packed down from people walking over it the past few days. It is nice and solid and I can hear our every step. Crunch, crunch, crunch. I can only hear our steps. Everything else is quiet.

We continue walking and come to a little trail that veers off and runs along the water. We head down the little trail and my husband notices something in the water. It looks like an otter swimming towards us, with his little head bobbing up and down, on his journey to shore. He keeps swimming towards us and Lou notices him. She wants to get to him and her body perks up. The otter spots Lou and quickly disappears in the water, leaving little ripples behind.

We continue to the small downtown street where all the stores are closed for the day. We walk along the street and take pictures of the ice sculptures that are lit up with changing colours. It's incredibly beautiful.

We return to the waterfront and walk back along the trail. There is no one on the trail but us.

It's dark. The sun has gone to sleep. All the ducks have retreated to a cove for the night. Thousands of ducks sit on the shore and some float in the water. We stop and listen. Nothing but nature making its peaceful hum in the night. I can see my breath. It is cold but I'm warm. I look up at the sky, so clear. In the distance the mountain is brightly lit. I feel a tremendous sense of peace from the stillness of the night.

"This is all there is," I say to my husband. "There is nothing else. Why is everyone scrambling around trying to find something other than this?" James feels it, too.

The gift of the moment. Peace.

Appendix A:

Little Laura

A FEW CONVERSATIONS WITH MY LITTLE GIRL. The real brave one.

Hi Little Laura. Thank you for telling me your story. I think it was hard that no one believed you. I cannot believe you had to hold it in. That is not right.

He was very scary. You did very well. I am here for you and love you. It's okay now. He was a bad person and I know how mean he was to you. But, I have become a good person because you have been so strong. I am so proud of you. Thank you for sharing your feelings. I feel very privileged to hear how you feel. I love you.

Sent Letters

Hi Little Laura. How are you feeling today?

Why?

Yes you did and I am so proud of you. Maybe now we can feel much better. It's hard to keep secrets, isn't it?.

Well, it is good to be brave and you have told the truth. Finally. It was good to do that. It was scary, I know. But you and I did it.

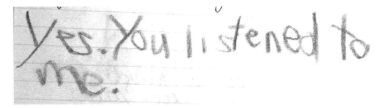

Yes. You listened to me.

I'm so sorry that I denied your feelings and stayed with my abuser. But now it's different.

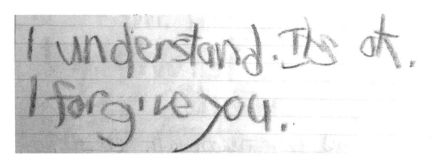

I understand. It's ok. I forgive you.

Thank you. You are making me cry again. You are an unbelievable little girl.

***

Hi Little Laura. I'm sad about Mom. How do you feel she's not talking to us?

She always believed him. So I don't care.

I know. He threatened to kill you. And she didn't get mad?

Good Lord. That is crazy. I'm shocked. I thought she'd come through. It's been hard dealing with the truth. It's been scary confronting the abuser. But we are healing. We are getting better.

I am finally listening. Love you so much.

Appendix B:

My Research

It has been extremely enlightening for me to research mental illness, child abuse and neglect. I have learned so much. There has been a lot of research on these subjects. I hope that mental illness doesn't have the stigma it once did. We need to become aware of how we can change things. With the internet, people are becoming more and more resourceful. And also, we are learning new therapies and strategies that are helping our children every day.

RESEARCH ON
PSYCHOLOGICAL ABUSE IN CHILDREN

Child protective service case workers may have a harder time recognizing and substantiating emotional neglect and abuse because there are no physical wounds. Also, psychological abuse isn't considered a serious social taboo like physical and sexual child abuse. We need public awareness initiatives to help people understand just how harmful psychological maltreatment is for children and adolescents.

— Joseph Spinazzola, *PhD, The Trauma Center at Justice Resource Institute, Brookline, Massachusetts*

Psychological abuse deserves some much-needed attention. Sexual and physical abuse have been receiving a lot of attention in recent years, which is extremely important. Now, it's time to talk about psychological abuse.

No physical signs. Psychological abuse is hidden and very hard to recognize, however it is every bit as damaging as physical and sexual abuse. The American Psychological Association (APA) revisited a study that was published in the *Psychological Trauma: Theory, Research, Practice, and Policy* publication in 2014. The APA paper was titled: *Unseen Wounds: The Contribution of Psychological Maltreatment to Child and Adolescent Mental Health and Risk Outcomes*[1].

What the study confirmed was that children who experienced psychological maltreatment were dealing with the same, or perhaps even worse, mental health problems than those children that had experienced physical and sexual abuse. The study also found that children who experienced psychological abuse experienced post-traumatic stress disorder just as often as children experiencing other forms of maltreatment and abuse. The paper concluded that there was a need for greater attention on psychological maltreatment.

Being a victim of psychological abuse, I couldn't agree more.

What are symptoms of psychological abuse in children?

Children who have experienced this type of abuse may have symptoms of the following: eating disorders; low self-esteem; anxiety and depression; withdrawal from society; rebellious conduct; sleep problems; physical complaints; and attempts at suicide. Being a victim, I have experienced many of these symptoms.

Recognizing the signs and seeking help from a healthcare professional is a great first step. Psychotherapy has many therapies that can greatly assist and benefit both children of child abuse and adult survivors.

For my recovery, therapy, mindfulness, journaling and Emotional Freedom Techniques were all extremely helpful in making me a survivor.

What I have learned is that it is okay to seek help and talk about abuse.

RESEARCH ON
EARLY CHILDHOOD ATTACHMENT

You can talk to most psychologists and they will tell you that the quality of love, from at least one primary caregiver, for a child up to three-years-old, will have a tremendous impact on that youngster. In 1969, psychologist John Bowlby developed the term the "Attachment Theory". The theory emphasizes that a strong emotional and physical attachment is critical to a child's growth in early years. The attachment gives the child security and a solid foundation. Without those attachments, children will become fearful. Children will be less likely to seek and learn new experiences, and there is a high risk for low empathy.

For over a half a century, psychologists have been researching the theory of attachment. It is an interesting subject that continues to be explored.

I am grateful that my son was rocked and held in my arms when he was an infant. He was given security from both parents. Holding my son was natural for me. For many years, it was believed you would "spoil" a child if you held them too much. Studies are now telling us differently.

What I have learned is how important bonding and attachment is to a young child.

RESEARCH ON
ADVERSE CHILDHOOD EXPERIENCES

What are Adverse Childhood Experiences (ACEs)? These are the traumatic childhood experiences that have potentially lasting, negative effects on a person's health and well-being in their adult years. There are two big factors that determine ACEs. One – Abuse. And Two – Neglect. Abuse being physical, emotional and sexual. Neglect being emotional and physical.

The *CDC-Kaiser Permanente Adverse Childhood Experiences Study*[2] was one of the largest examinations on child abuse and neglect. It focused on the long-term effects of child abuse and neglect on a person's health and well-being when they are adults. What the major findings show is that as the number of ACEs increase, so does the risk of the following that are listed on the Centers for Disease Control and Prevention website:

- Disrupted neurodevelopment
- Social, emotional and cognitive impairment
- Adoption of health-risk behaviours
- Disease, disability and social problems
- Early death

The study concluded the link between childhood trauma and adults having chronic diseases with social and emotional problems. This is only one study.

What I have learned is that research now shows strong links between childhood abuse and neglect resulting in later-life health problems and challenges to well-being.

[1] https://www.apa.org/pubs/journals/releases/tra-a0037766.pdf
[2] https://www.cdc.gov/violenceprevention/acestudy/about.html

Please visit **www.lauracorbeth.com** to read and follow her blog.

Printed in Great Britain
by Amazon

44060582R00136